# SIX SISTERS' STUFF

# instant cooking

SIX SISTERS' STUFF

# instant cooking

A FAST, EASY, AND DELICIOUS WAY TO FEED YOUR FAMILY

SHADOW
MOUNTAIN

To our sister Kristen,

the multicooker queen,

who taught us all to use and love our pressure cookers!

All photographs courtesy Six Sisters' Stuff

Any trademarks, service marks, product names, or named features are the property of their respective owners, and they are used herein for reference and comparison purposes only. This book was not prepared, approved, licensed, or endorsed by any of the owners of the trademarks or brand names referred to in this book. There is no express or implied endorsement for any products or services mentioned in this publication.

Visit us at ShadowMountain.com

Instant Pot® is the registered trademark of its owner. Shadow Mountain Publishing, LLC is not associated with or sponsored by Instant Pot.

Library of Congress Cataloging-in-Publication Data

Names: Six Sisters' Stuff.
Title: Instant cooking : a fast, easy, and delicious way to feed your family / Six Sisters' Stuff.
Description: Salt Lake City, Utah : Shadow Mountain, [2021] | Includes index. | Summary: "The Six Sisters continue their ongoing series of cookbooks with recipes and tips for using an electronic multicooker"—Provided by publisher.
Identifiers: LCCN 2020027806 | ISBN 9781629727912 (paperback)
Subjects: LCSH: Smart cookers. | LCGFT: Cookbooks.
Classification: LCC TX840.S63 I57 2021 | DDC 641.5/87—dc23
LC record available at https://lccn.loc.gov/2020027806

Printed in China
RR Donnelley, Dongguan, China

10  9  8  7  6  5  4  3  2  1

# contents

## SIDE DISHES

## DESSERTS AND SNACKS

# INTRODUCTION

Dear reader and multicooker chef,

Welcome to *Instant Cooking with Six Sisters' Stuff*! We hope you enjoy the recipes we've collected here as much as we do. Instant cooking is a real gift in our sometimes too-scheduled lives.

We thought we'd introduce this book with some common-sense instructions about instant cooking.

First, it's not *really* instant. Multicookers like the Instant Pot and other brands are actually electronically controlled pressure cookers, and the addition of pressure to heat makes them able to do a lot of things quickly that would take longer via a traditional method (like roasting meat, for example). But because multicookers must first pressurize their contents, some processes (like soft- or hard-boiling eggs) take about the same amount of time overall, because some time is taken getting the cooker up to either high or low pressure. However, much of the time, as is the case with hard-boiling eggs, there are definite advantages to the instant cooking method—fewer ruptured eggs and easier-peeling shells, to name two.

Second, there are several varieties and brands of multicooker on the market. The recipes here were tested on a 6-quart Instant Pot Duo, though some would work best in an 8-quart multicooker. The functions on most multicookers are similar, but might not be the same as described here. Make sure you know your multicooker's functions well before beginning. Some recipes might take a little tweaking to make the best use of your particular multicooker's functions.

Third, some of the recipes require accessories beyond those that usually are included with a multicooker. These make the multicooker much more useful. The accessories we've used include:

- A 7-inch springform pan for cheesecakes, brownies, or other cakes
- 7-inch cake pans, including stackable pans for cakes as well as for cooking separate ingredients at the same time
- Loaf pans for breads
- A glass lid to use when not bringing the pot to pressure

- An extra silicone sealing ring. After a little use, the silicone sealing rings can retain the flavors of what's been cooked. Having separate rings for cooking sweet or savory foods keeps your cakes from tasting like garlic.
- An extra insert (for making dinner in one and dessert in the other)
- A silicone egg bites mold, handy for making not only egg bites but other small molded bites—like brownies!
- Special mitts for handling hot inserts
- Trivets and steamer inserts

Fourth, using a multicooker means taking safety seriously. Some tips we've learned (some through experience) include:

- Pressurized cooking means that when something's done, the pressure has to be released before the lid can be removed—and pressurized steam is involved. Multicookers have a pressure release valve, and there are two ways to release the pressure. A "natural" release means that you leave the pot in warming mode (which it switches to when the timer has expired) for several minutes and the pressure releases slowly and naturally. Some recipes will call for a natural release (or a specific natural-release time, such as 15 minutes). The other type of release is a "quick" release, where you open the pressure valve as soon as the timer is done. Covering the valve with a towel or using a wooden spoon to carefully open it so that the escaping steam doesn't burn your hand or arm is a good idea. It's also a good idea to have your multicooker on a surface where steam escaping above the pot isn't going to warp your cookbook collection or inadvertently melt your stash of chocolate.
- Pressurized cooking also means that you should always remember to switch the valve to "sealing" before setting the pressure and the timer. If the valve isn't closed, the multicooker will still try to get the pot to pressure, but steam will release through the open valve. This can burn what you're cooking if not caught in time, and will likely not cook things well even if caught relatively early.
- Inside the lid of your multicooker is a silicone ring that must be in place for the lid to seal. If your lid won't close, it's likely because the seal is somehow out of place.
- Recipes that call for removing trivets, steamer baskets, or stackable pans can be made easier by using a homemade aluminum-foil sling underneath. A length of foil about four times longer than your insert is tall, folded lengthwise in fourths, can be placed in the insert before the pans

or baskets and then folded over the top before beginning to cook. Once the lid is off, using oven mitts, you can use the sling to pull the pan clear of the insert.

- Most multicookers will display an error (or "burn") message if food gets stuck to the bottom of the insert. This can happen if you don't have enough liquid in the pot (at least 1 cup of a thin liquid), if you've stirred together thick liquids (recipes with, for instance, beef broth and tomato sauce should add the broth, then the solid ingredients, then the sauce directly on top without mixing, then pressure cook, *then* mix), or if you've used milk or cream directly (sauces like alfredo sauce should be cooked in a separate pan within the insert so they don't scald to the bottom of the insert and cause a burn message).

All that said, our multicookers have been amazing. We hope that these recipes will show you just how much a multicooker can bless your life.

—The Six Sisters

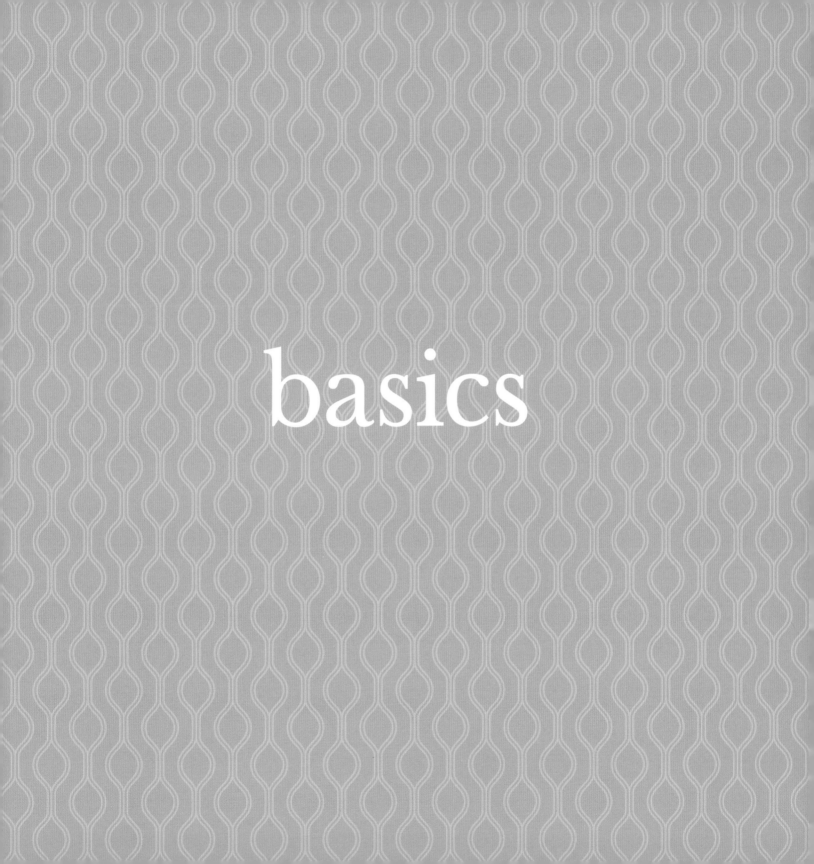

# basics

# STEAMED BROCCOLI

Prep time: 1 minute | Pressurization and cooking time: 7 to 9 minutes | Total time: 8 to 10 minutes | Yields: 4 servings

½ cup water

**2 to 3 cups broccoli florets**

1. Pour ½ cup water into the insert of a multicooker.

2. Place steamer basket in the insert.

3. Place broccoli in steamer basket.

4. Secure the lid and make sure the valve is pointing up to SEALING.

5. Press MANUAL (or press PRESSURE COOK and select HIGH PRESSURE) and adjust time to 0 minutes (bringing the multicooker to pressure will cook the broccoli perfectly).

6. When multicooker signals the end of cooking time, press CANCEL, and then quick release the pressure by turning the valve down to VENTING with the handle of a wooden spoon or other device to prevent the steam from burning your hands during the release.

7. Season with salt and pepper and serve.

# CARROTS

Prep time: 1 minute | Pressurization and cooking time: 7 to 9 minutes | Total time: 8 to 10 minutes | Yields: 4 servings

1 cup cold water

1 pound baby carrots

1. Pour 1 cup water in the insert of a multicooker.

2. Place steamer rack in the insert.

3. Place carrots on top of the steamer rack.

4. Secure the lid and make sure the valve is pointing up to SEALING.

5. Press MANUAL (or press PRESSURE COOK and select HIGH PRESSURE) and adjust time to 2 minutes.

6. When multicooker signals the end of cooking time, press CANCEL, and then quick release the pressure by turning the valve down to VENTING with the handle of a wooden spoon or other device to prevent the steam from burning your hands during the release.

7. Remove the carrots, season as desired, and serve.

# CORN ON THE COB

Prep time: 5 minutes | Pressurization and cooking time: 12 to 14 minutes | Total time: 17 to 19 minutes | Yields: 6 servings

**6** **ears corn, husks and silk removed**

**1** **cup water**

1. Pour water into the insert of a multicooker.

2. Place trivet in the bottom of the insert.

3. Place 2 to 3 ears of corn on top of the trivet. Stack 2 to 3 more ears of corn on top and perpendicular to those.

4. Secure the lid and make sure the valve is pointing up to SEALING.

5. Press MANUAL (or press PRESSURE COOK and select HIGH PRESSURE) and adjust time to 2 minutes.

6. When multicooker signals the end of cooking time, press CANCEL, and then quick release the pressure by turning the valve down to VENTING with the handle of a wooden spoon or other device to prevent the steam from burning your hands during the release.

7. Remove lid and use tongs to remove hot corn from multicooker. Slather with butter, season with salt and pepper, and enjoy.

# GREEN BEANS

Prep time: 4 minutes | Pressurization and cooking time: 7 minutes | Total time: 11 minutes | Yields: 4 servings

---

1 **cup water**

1 **pound fresh green beans, ends trimmed**

1 **tablespoon butter, melted**

**Salt and pepper, to taste**

1. Pour 1 cup water in the insert of a multicooker and then place the steamer rack in the insert.

2. Place green beans on top of the steamer rack.

3. Secure the lid and make sure the valve is pointing up to SEALING.

4. Press MANUAL and select LOW PRESSURE (or press PRESSURE COOK and select LOW PRESSURE) and adjust time to 1 minute. For firmer green beans, set time to 0; for softer green beans, set time to 2 minutes.

5. When multicooker signals the end of cooking time, press CANCEL, and then quick release the pressure by turning the valve down to VENTING with the handle of a wooden spoon or other device to prevent the steam from burning your hands during the release.

6. Open lid carefully and transfer green beans from the insert to a medium bowl. Toss beans with melted butter, season with salt and pepper, and serve immediately.

# BAKED POTATOES

Prep time: 2 minutes | Pressurization and cooking time: 35 to 40 minutes | Total time: 37 to 42 minutes | Yields: 4 to 5 servings

**4 to 5 medium russet potatoes, scrubbed clean**

**1 cup water**

1. Stab each potato with a fork 5 to 8 times.

2. Pour 1 cup water into the insert of a multicooker.

3. Place steamer basket or trivet in the bottom of insert.

4. Place potatoes on top of the trivet or inside the steamer basket.

5. Secure the lid and make sure the valve is pointing up to SEALING.

6. Press MANUAL (or press PRESSURE COOK and select HIGH PRESSURE) and adjust time to 12 minutes.

7. When multicooker signals the end of cooking time, let pressure naturally release 15 minutes.

8. Remove from insert and serve immediately with desired toppings. Alternatively, let potatoes cool, place in an airtight container and refrigerate 3 to 4 days.

# SWEET POTATOES

Prep time: 2 minutes | Pressurization and cooking time: 25 to 40 minutes, depending on size of potatoes | Total time: 27 to 42 minutes | Yields: 4 servings

1   **cup water**

4   **sweet potatoes, scrubbed and rinsed**

1. Pour 1 cup water into the insert of a multicooker.

2. Place trivet in the bottom of the insert.

3. Pierce each potato 5 to 6 times with a fork. This allows for steam to escape from the potatoes while they cook.

4. Arrange sweet potatoes on top of the trivet. Secure the lid and make sure the valve is pointing up to SEALING.

5. Press MANUAL (or press PRESSURE COOK and select HIGH PRESSURE) and adjust time to 15 minutes for small potatoes (about 2 inches in diameter), 22 for medium potatoes (about 3 inches in diameter), or 30 for large potatoes (about 4 inches in diameter).

6. When multicooker signals the end of cooking time, let pressure naturally release for 10 minutes.

7. Quick release any remaining pressure and carefully remove sweet potatoes from the multicooker.

8. Serve and enjoy!

*Note: If you have large potatoes but want them to cook in a shorter amount of time, cut the potatoes in half before placing them in the multicooker to cook.*

# RICE

Prep time: 1 minute | Pressurization and cooking time: 22 to 27 minutes | Total time: 27 to 28 minutes | Yields: 4 servings

**1** cup long grain or jasmine rice, rinsed well

**1¼** cups water

1. Put rice in the insert of a multicooker and cover with 1¼ cups water.

2. Secure the lid and make sure the valve is pointing up to SEALING.

3. Press RICE or MANUAL (or press PRESSURE COOK and select HIGH PRESSURE) and adjust time to 7 minutes.

4. When multicooker signals the end of cooking time, let pressure naturally release 10 minutes. Turn valve to VENTING to release any remaining pressure.

5. Remove lid, fluff rice with a fork, and serve.

*Note: Any kind of rice can be cooked in the multicooker. Simply adjust the time in step 3 according to the type of rice you are using: 6 to 8 minutes for basmati rice; 22 to 24 minutes for brown rice; 25 to 30 minutes for wild rice.*

# PASTA

Prep time: 1 minute | Pressurization and cooking time: 11 minutes | Total time: 12 minutes | Yields: 6 servings

**1   pound pasta**

**4   cups water**

**½   teaspoon salt**

1. Place pasta in the insert of a multicooker and cover with water. Stir in salt.

2. Secure the lid and make sure the valve is pointing up to SEALING.

3. Press MANUAL (or press PRESSURE COOK and select HIGH PRESSURE) and adjust time to 4 minutes.

4. When multicooker signals the end of cooking time, let pressure naturally release 5 minutes. After 5 minutes, turn the valve to VENTING to release any remaining pressure.

5. Remove and drain pasta, then use it in your favorite recipes.

# OATMEAL

Prep time: 1 minute | Pressurization and cooking time: 10 to 12 minutes | Total time: 13 to 15 minutes | Yields: 4 servings

---

2   **cups old fashioned oats**

4   **cups water**

1. Mix oats and water together in the insert of a multicooker.

2. Secure the lid and make sure the valve is pointing up to SEALING.

3. Press MANUAL (or press PRESSURE COOK and select HIGH PRESSURE) and adjust time to 4 minutes.

4. When multicooker signals the end of cooking time, press CANCEL, and then quick release the pressure by turning the valve down to VENTING with the handle of a wooden spoon or other device to prevent the steam from burning your hands during the release.

5. Top as desired for a tasty and filling breakfast.

# COLD-START, NO-BOIL MULTICOOKER YOGURT

Prep time: 5 minutes | Cooking and chilling time: 12 to 20 hours, depending on desired thickness | Total time: 12 hours 5 minutes, or more | Yields: 10 to 12 servings

---

1 (52-ounce) carton ultra-pasteurized, ultra-high temperature, or shelf stable milk, such as Fairlife milk

1 (14-ounce) can sweetened condensed milk (optional)

1 to 2 tablespoons plain or vanilla yogurt

1. Pour milk into the insert of a multicooker.

2. Stir in the sweetened condensed milk, if using, and whisk well.

3. Whisk in 1 to 2 tablespoons yogurt.

4. Secure the lid and make sure the valve is pointing up to SEALING.

5. Press YOGURT and adjust the incubation time to at least 8 hours. You can increase the incubation time up to 24 hours if you want a tangier yogurt. (Note that the timer counts up while the yogurt incubates.)

6. When the multicooker signals the end of cooking time, the display will read YOGT. Remove the insert with the yogurt still in it, cover, and chill in the refrigerator 4 to 6 hours. (Do not stir yogurt until fully chilled or strained.)

7. For regular yogurt, skip this step and move to step 8. For a thicker, Greek-like yogurt, strain chilled yogurt by lining a fine sieve with cheesecloth, a coffee filter, or a paper towel and setting the sieve over a bowl. Spoon yogurt into sieve and refrigerate the bowl and sieve together 2 hours to allow the liquid to drain off.

8. Transfer yogurt to a bowl and stir. Add any desired flavorings.

9. Store, covered, in the refrigerator up to 2 weeks.

# main dishes

# CHICKEN POT PIE

Prep time: 20 minutes | Pressurization and cooking time: 1 hour 15 minutes | Total time: 1 hour 35 minutes | Yields: 6 to 8 servings

---

3 frozen chicken breasts

1 cup chicken broth, divided

1 onion, chopped

3 large potatoes, peeled and chopped

1 (10-ounce) package frozen mixed vegetables

1⅔ cup Red Lobster Cheddar Bay Biscuit Mix

⅓ cup milk

⅓ cup shredded cheddar cheese

1 teaspoon Italian seasoning

Salt and pepper, to taste

2 puff pastry sheets, thawed

1. Place frozen chicken breasts in the insert of a multicooker and pour ½ cup of the broth over the top.

2. Secure the lid and make sure the valve is pointing up to SEALING.

3. Press MANUAL (or press PRESSURE COOK and select HIGH PRESSURE) and adjust time to 20 minutes.

4. When multicooker signals the end of cooking time, press CANCEL, and then quick release the pressure by turning the valve down to VENTING with the handle of a wooden spoon or other device to prevent the steam from burning your hands during the release.

5. Remove lid and shred the chicken in the insert with 2 forks.

6. Add remaining ½ cup broth, onion, potatoes, and frozen vegetables and stir well to combine with shredded chicken.

7. Secure the lid and make sure the valve is pointing up to SEALING.

8. Press MANUAL (or press PRESSURE COOK and select HIGH PRESSURE) and adjust time to 3 minutes.

9. While vegetables are cooking, prepare biscuits: In a medium bowl, combine biscuit mix, milk, and cheese just until dough forms; do not overmix. Shape dough into 15–20 small balls.

10. When multicooker signals the end of cooking time, press CANCEL, and then quick release the pressure by turning the valve down to VENTING with the handle of a wooden spoon or other device to prevent the steam from burning your hands during the release.

11. Remove lid, press SAUTÉ, and then add biscuit balls to the chicken and vegetables.

12. Let biscuits cook 4 minutes, then turn them over and cook another 4 minutes.

13. Break up biscuits with a wooden spoon and mix into chicken and vegetables. This pot pie filling will be very thick.

14. Preheat oven to 350 degrees F.

15. Unfold 1 thawed puff pastry sheet and lay it on the counter. Flip over an 8-inch round cake pan or pie tin and place it on top of the puff pastry. Trim a circle around the pan, leaving an inch around the edges. Repeat with second puff pastry sheet.

16. Divide filling equally between 2 (8-inch) round cake pans or pie tins. Cover each with prepared puff pastry sheet and fold under edges.

17. Bake 10 to 15 minutes, until pastry has puffed up and turned golden brown.

18. Let pies cool 5 to 10 minutes before cutting and serving.

# CREAMY TOMATO CHICKEN

Prep time: 20 minutes | Pressurization and cooking time: 25 to 30 minutes | Total time: 45 to 50 minutes | Yields: 4 servings

½  teaspoon garlic powder

1  teaspoon paprika, divided

2  teaspoons Italian seasoning, divided

1  teaspoon salt, divided

4  boneless skinless chicken breasts

2  teaspoons butter, divided

1  teaspoon olive oil

1  onion, chopped

1  tablespoon minced garlic

¼  cup white wine vinegar

2  cups unsalted tomato sauce

½  teaspoon ground black pepper

½  cup heavy cream

6  green onions, finely sliced

4  cups hot, cooked rice, mashed potatoes, or pasta

1. In a shallow bowl, stir together garlic powder, ½ teaspoon paprika, ½ teaspoon Italian seasoning, and ½ teaspoon salt.

2. Coat chicken breasts with seasoning and set aside.

3. Add 1 teaspoon butter and the oil to the insert of a multicooker and press SAUTÉ.

4. When oil and butter are hot and begin to ripple, place the seasoned chicken in the multicooker and let it brown 2 minutes on one side. Flip the chicken and let it brown another 2 minutes. Remove the chicken and set aside.

5. Add remaining butter to the pot, followed by chopped onion and garlic. Sauté onion and garlic 1 to 2 minutes, until onion begins to soften.

6. Pour white wine vinegar into pot and use a spatula to deglaze the bottom of the insert, releasing any stuck browned bits.

7. Add tomato sauce, remaining 1½ teaspoons Italian seasoning, ½ teaspoon paprika, ½ teaspoon salt, and pepper to the insert. Stir well.

8. Press CANCEL and then place the browned chicken in a single layer in the multicooker.

9. Secure the lid and make sure the valve is pointing up to SEALING.

10. Press MANUAL (or press PRESSURE COOK and select HIGH PRESSURE) and adjust time to 5 minutes.

11. When multicooker signals the end of cooking time, let pressure naturally release 10 minutes. Turn valve to VENTING to quick release any remaining pressure.

12. Press CANCEL and remove the lid. Transfer chicken to a large bowl and shred with 2 forks. Return chicken to multicooker.

13. Press SAUTÉ and then stir in the cream and mix everything well to coat the chicken with the sauce. Stir until sauce looks creamy and chicken is coated well.

14. Press CANCEL to turn off multicooker and serve the chicken and creamy tomato sauce over hot cooked rice, mashed potatoes, or pasta.

# HONEY-GARLIC CHICKEN

Prep time: 10 minutes | Pressurization and cooking time: 20 minutes | Total time: 30 minutes | Yields: 6 servings

---

| | | | | |
|---|---|---|---|---|
| 3 | boneless, skinless chicken breasts | | 1 | tablespoon minced garlic |
| | Salt and pepper, to taste | | ½ | onion, diced |
| ½ | cup honey | | ¼ | cup water plus 1 tablespoon, divided |
| ⅓ | cup ketchup | | 1 | tablespoon cornstarch |
| ¼ | cup brown sugar | | 6 | cups hot, cooked rice |
| ⅓ | cup soy sauce | | | Sesame seeds, for garnishing |
| 2 | tablespoons vegetable oil | | | Chopped green onions, for garnishing |

1. Season chicken with salt and pepper and set aside.

2. In a small mixing bowl, whisk together honey, ketchup, brown sugar, soy sauce, vegetable oil, garlic, onion, and ¼ cup water.

3. Arrange chicken in the insert of a multicooker and pour sauce over the top.

4. Secure the lid and make sure the valve is pointing up to SEALING.

5. Press MANUAL (or press PRESSURE COOK and select HIGH PRESSURE) and adjust time to 20 minutes.

6. When multicooker signals the end of cooking time, press CANCEL, and then quick release the pressure by turning the valve down to VENTING with the handle of a wooden spoon or other device to prevent the steam from burning your hands during the release.

7. Remove chicken from the multicooker and cut into bite-sized pieces; set aside.

8. In a small bowl, whisk together 1 tablespoon water and cornstarch; whisk cornstarch into the sauce in the multicooker.

9. Press SAUTÉ and cook 5 minutes, stirring constantly until thickened.

10. Press CANCEL and fold in cooked chicken.

11. Serve chicken and sauce over rice, and garnish with sesame seeds and green onion.

# SESAME CHICKEN

Prep time: 10 minutes | Pressurization and cooking time: 15 minutes | Total time: 25 minutes | Yields: 6 servings

3   tablespoons cornstarch, divided

Salt and pepper, to taste

1½  pounds boneless skinless chicken breasts or thighs, cut into pieces

2   tablespoons sesame oil, divided

¾   cup low-sodium soy sauce

¼   cup ketchup

Pinch red pepper flakes

6   tablespoons honey

3   tablespoons water

3 to 4 cups hot, cooked rice

1   tablespoon sesame seeds

1. In a gallon-sized resealable bag, mix together 2 tablespoons of the cornstarch with salt and pepper.

2. Add chicken pieces to bag, seal, and shake until chicken is completely coated with cornstarch. If needed, add more cornstarch to ensure all chicken is covered.

3. Pour 1½ tablespoons of the sesame oil into the insert of a multicooker and press SAUTÉ.

4. When oil is hot and begins to ripple, add chicken pieces and sauté 3 to 4 minutes, until all sides of the chicken begin to turn golden-brown.

5. When chicken has browned, press CANCEL.

6. In a small bowl, mix together soy sauce, ketchup, and red pepper flakes. Pour over chicken pieces and stir gently so that all the chicken pieces are covered in sauce.

7. Secure the lid and make sure the valve is pointing up to SEALING.

8. Press MANUAL (or press PRESSURE COOK and select HIGH PRESSURE) and adjust time to 3 minutes.

9. When multicooker signals the end of cooking time, press CANCEL, and then quick release the pressure by turning the valve down to VENTING with the handle of a wooden spoon or other device to prevent the steam from burning your hands during the release.

10. Remove lid and stir in honey and remaining ½ tablespoon sesame oil.

11. In a small bowl, mix together water and remaining 1 tablespoon cornstarch. Pour cornstarch mixture over chicken and stir gently.

12. Press SAUTÉ and cook, stirring occasionally, until sauce thickens, about 2 to 3 minutes.

13. Serve over hot, cooked rice and top with sesame seeds.

# CHEESY CHICKEN AND RICE

Prep time: 15 minutes | Pressurization and cooking time: 18 to 20 minutes | Total time: 33 to 40 minutes | Yields: 6 servings

1½ pounds boneless skinless chicken breasts, cut into bite-sized pieces

2 tablespoons olive oil

1 teaspoon salt

1 teaspoon ground black pepper

1 onion, diced

3 cloves garlic, minced

2 cups long grain white rice

1 (15-ounce) can low-sodium chicken broth

½ cup water

1 (10.5-ounce) can cream of chicken soup

2 cups shredded cheddar cheese

1 (10-ounce) bag frozen mixed vegetables

1. Pour olive oil into the insert of a multicooker and press SAUTÉ.

2. When oil is heated and begins to ripple, add chicken pieces, salt, pepper, onion, and garlic. Sauté until onions become translucent and chicken starts to brown, about 5 to 7 minutes.

3. Stir in rice and sauté 1 to 2 minutes more, just until rice begins to turn golden brown.

4. Press CANCEL and then stir in chicken broth and water.

5. Secure the lid and make sure the valve is pointing up to SEALING.

6. Press MANUAL (or press PRESSURE COOK and select HIGH PRESSURE) and adjust time to 8 minutes.

7. When multicooker signals the end of cooking time, quick release the pressure by turning the valve down to VENTING with the handle of a wooden spoon or other device to prevent the steam from burning your hands during the release.

8. Remove lid and stir in soup, shredded cheese, and frozen vegetables. Mix until cheese is melted, and vegetables are warmed through.

# CHICKEN TIKKA MASALA

Prep time: 1 hour 5 minutes (or more if marinating overnight) | Pressurization and cooking time: 35 minutes | Total time: 1 hour 40 minutes (or more if marinating overnight) | Yields: 4 to 6

1 cup plain, 2-percent fat Greek yogurt

1 tablespoon plus 4 teaspoons garam masala, divided

1 tablespoon lemon juice

1 teaspoon ground black pepper

¼ teaspoon ground ginger

1 pound boneless skinless chicken breasts, chopped into bite-sized pieces

1 (15-ounce) can tomato sauce or puree

5 cloves garlic, minced

½ teaspoon paprika

½ teaspoon ground turmeric

½ teaspoon salt

¼ teaspoon cayenne pepper

1 cup heavy cream

4 cups hot, cooked white rice

Chopped cilantro, for topping

1. In a gallon-size zipper-top bag, add yogurt, 4 teaspoons garam masala, lemon juice, pepper, and ginger. Add chicken pieces, seal bag, and shake well to coat chicken. Refrigerate at least 1 hour or overnight.

2. When ready to prepare Tikka Masala, remove chicken from refrigerator. Press SAUTÉ to heat the insert of a multicooker. When pot is hot, use tongs to transfer marinated chicken from bag to the insert, shaking chicken pieces gently as you do so to allow excess marinade to drip back into bag. Discard marinade. Sauté until chicken is cooked on all sides, stirring occasionally, about 8 minutes. Press CANCEL.

3. Add tomato sauce, garlic, remaining 1 tablespoon garam masala, paprika, turmeric, salt, and cayenne; stir to combine with chicken.

4. Secure the lid and make sure the valve is pointing up to SEALING.

5. Press MANUAL (or press PRESSURE COOK and select HIGH PRESSURE) and adjust time to 10 minutes.

6. When multicooker signals the end of cooking time, press CANCEL, and then quick release the pressure by turning the valve down to VENTING with the handle of a wooden spoon or other device to prevent the steam from burning your hands during the release.

7. Remove lid and press SAUTÉ. Stir in cream and simmer until the sauce is thickened, about 3 minutes.

8. Serve over hot, cooked rice, garnished with chopped cilantro.

# SHREDDED CHICKEN TACOS

Prep time: 5 minutes | Pressurization and cooking time: 45 minutes | Total time: 50 minutes | Yields: 10 soft tacos

---

| | | | | |
|---|---|---|---|---|
| 5 | boneless, skinless chicken breasts | | 10 | soft taco flour tortillas |
| 1 | tablespoon chili powder | | | Favorite taco toppings, such as shredded cheese, chopped tomatoes, shredded lettuce, salsa, and sour cream |
| 1 | tablespoon ground cumin | | | |
| ½ | cup water | | | |

1. Place chicken breasts in the bottom of the multicooker insert.

2. Sprinkle chili powder and cumin over chicken breasts and then pour the water over the spices.

3. Secure the lid and make sure the valve is pointing up to SEALING.

4. Press MANUAL (or press PRESSURE COOK and select HIGH PRESSURE) and adjust time to 20 minutes for thawed chicken breasts or 25 minutes for frozen chicken breasts.

5. When multicooker signals the end of cooking time, let pressure naturally release 10 minutes and then carefully turn the valve to VENTING to quick release remaining pressure.

6. Remove lid, transfer chicken to a large bowl, and shred with a fork.

7. Return shredded chicken to the multicooker insert and stir it into the liquid until thoroughly coated.

8. Serve in tortillas topped with your favorite taco toppings.

# CHICKEN ENCHILADA LASAGNA

Prep time: 10 minutes | Pressurization and cooking time: 20 minutes | Total time: 30 minutes | Yields: 4 servings

1    (14-ounce) can enchilada sauce

4    corn tortillas

1    cup cubed or shredded cooked chicken

2    cups shredded mozzarella cheese

½    cup water

Chopped tomatoes, chopped avocado, and sour cream, for topping

1. Layer lasagna ingredients in a multicooker pan, such as the double stack Ekovana brand pan: Spread 2 spoonsful enchilada sauce on the bottom of the pan. Place a tortilla on top of the sauce, tearing the tortilla to make it fit, if needed. Spread 1/3 cup of the chicken over the tortilla and cover with ½ cup of the shredded mozzarella. Repeat until all tortillas are used, ending with remaining sauce and cheese. Cover pan with foil or lid, if it has one.

2. Pour ½ cup water in the insert of a multicooker and carefully place covered pan inside the insert.

3. Secure the lid and make sure the valve is pointing up to SEALING.

4. Press MANUAL (or press PRESSURE COOK and select HIGH PRESSURE) and adjust time to 3 minutes.

5. When multicooker signals the end of cooking time, press CANCEL, and then quick release the pressure by turning the valve down to VENTING with the handle of a wooden spoon or other device to prevent the steam from burning your hands during the release.

6. Remove the lid and carefully take out the pan.

7. Heat oven to broil and gently remove foil or lid from pan.

8. Broil until cheese turns golden brown, about 1 minute.

9. Serve hot, topped with chopped tomatoes, avocados, and sour cream.

# SPICY CHICKEN AND RICE BOWLS

Prep time: 5 minutes | Pressurization and cooking time: 20 minutes | Total time: 25 minutes | Yields: 4 to 6 servings

---

3   boneless skinless chicken breasts, diced

1   onion, roughly chopped

1   cup chicken broth

1   (15-ounce) can corn

1   (15-ounce) can kidney beans, rinsed and drained

1   (4.5-ounce) can green chilis

1   (1-ounce) packet taco seasoning

1   cup salsa

1   cup long grain white rice

1. Add chicken, onions, broth, corn, kidney beans, green chilis, taco seasoning, salsa, and rice to the insert of a multicooker.

2. Gently stir to make sure all the rice is touching the liquids, but don't mix too much.

3. Secure the lid and make sure the valve is pointing up to SEALING.

4. Press MANUAL (or press PRESSURE COOK and select HIGH PRESSURE) and adjust time to 9 minutes.

5. When multicooker signals the end of cooking time, press CANCEL, and then quick release the pressure by turning the valve down to VENTING with the handle of a wooden spoon or other device to prevent the steam from burning your hands during the release.

6. Remove the lid and stir to combine.

7. Serve with your favorite toppings, such as diced avocado, shredded cheese, chopped cilantro, sour cream, and so on.

# EASY TUSCAN CHICKEN PASTA

Prep time: 5 minutes | Pressurization and cooking time: 25 minutes | Total time: 30 minutes | Yields: 6 to 8 servings

2 cups cooked and diced chicken

2 cups ditalini or other small pasta

2 cups chicken broth

2 tablespoons butter

1 (8-ounce) brick cream cheese

½ cup milk

½ cup grated Parmesan cheese

4 ounces sun dried tomatoes, drained and chopped

½ teaspoon garlic salt

½ teaspoon ground black pepper

1 tablespoon dried basil

2 cups fresh spinach

1. Add chicken, pasta, broth, and butter to the insert of a multicooker.

2. Secure the lid and make sure the valve is pointing up to SEALING.

3. Press MANUAL (or press PRESSURE COOK and select HIGH PRESSURE) and adjust time to 3 minutes.

4. When multicooker signals the end of cooking time, let pressure naturally release 5 minutes and then carefully turn the valve to VENTING to quick release remaining pressure.

5. Press CANCEL, remove the lid, and stir the noodles and chicken.

6. Press SAUTÉ and stir in cream cheese, milk, Parmesan cheese, garlic salt, black pepper, and basil. Stir until cheese is melted.

7. Mix in the sun-dried tomatoes and spinach, stirring just until spinach is cooked down a bit and everything is well combined, about 2 minutes.

8. Serve hot with your favorite salad and breadsticks!

# BUFFALO CHICKEN WRAPS

Prep time: 5 minutes | Pressurization and cooking time: 15 minutes | Total time: 20 minutes | Yields: 4 servings

---

1 pound boneless chicken breasts

1 cup buffalo sauce, such as Frank's RedHot Wings Buffalo Sauce

1 (1-ounce) packet ranch dressing mix

½ cup chicken broth

4 flour tortillas

1 avocado, sliced

½ cup shredded carrots

1 cup shredded lettuce

1. Place chicken breasts, buffalo sauce, ranch dressing mix, and chicken broth in the insert of a multicooker.

2. Secure the lid and make sure the valve is pointing up to SEALING.

3. Press MANUAL (or press PRESSURE COOK and select HIGH PRESSURE) and adjust time to 10 minutes.

4. When multicooker signals the end of cooking time, press CANCEL, and let pressure naturally release for 5 minutes, then quick release the remaining pressure by turning the valve down to VENTING with the handle of a wooden spoon or other device to prevent the steam from burning your hands during the release.

5. Remove lid and transfer chicken to a cutting board or large bowl and shred with 2 forks. Return shredded chicken to sauce in multicooker and stir well.

6. Assemble wraps by layering chicken, sliced avocado, shredded carrots, and shredded lettuce on flour tortillas. Wrap and serve immediately.

# SEASONED TURKEY BREAST

Prep time: 15 minutes | Pressurization and cooking time: 35 to 40 minutes | Total time: 50 to 55 minutes | Yields: 6 to 8 servings

1 tablespoon smoked paprika

1 tablespoon Italian seasoning

1 teaspoon salt

2 teaspoons ground black pepper

2 cloves garlic, minced

1 tablespoon olive oil

1 (4-pound) turkey breast

½ cup water

1. In a small bowl, combine paprika, Italian seasoning, salt, pepper, and garlic.

2. Drizzle olive oil all over the turkey breast, rub it in, and then rub the spice mixture over all sides of the turkey breast; set aside.

3. Place trivet in the bottom of the multicooker insert. Pour ⅓ cup of water into the insert and place seasoned turkey on top of the trivet.

4. Secure the lid and make sure the valve is pointing up to SEALING.

5. Press MANUAL (or press PRESSURE COOK and select HIGH PRESSURE) and adjust time to 25 minutes.

6. When multicooker signals the end of cooking time, let pressure naturally release.

7. Remove lid and transfer the turkey breast to a cutting board. Cover turkey completely with aluminum foil and let it rest 10 to 15 minutes before slicing into it.

*Note: For crispier skin, place turkey breast on a baking sheet and broil in the oven 5 to 10 minutes.*

# HOMEMADE GROUND TURKEY PASTA SAUCE

Prep time: 10 minutes | Pressurization and cooking time: 30 to 35 minutes | Total time: 40 to 45 minutes | Yields: 8 servings

1 pound ground Italian turkey sausage

3 tablespoons minced onion flakes

4 teaspoons minced garlic

1 (28-ounce) can crushed tomatoes

1 (6-ounce) can tomato paste

1 cup water

2 tablespoons granulated sugar

1 tablespoon dried oregano

1 tablespoon dried basil

1 teaspoon fennel seed

1 teaspoon salt

½ teaspoon ground black pepper

1 (16-ounce) package pasta, such as penne, fettucine, or spaghetti, prepared according to package directions

Shredded Parmesan cheese, for topping

1. Press SAUTÉ to heat multicooker insert; add sausage and use a wooden spoon to break up meat and cook until browned, about 5 to 7 minutes.

2. Press CANCEL and then add onion flakes, minced garlic, crushed tomatoes, tomato paste, water, sugar, oregano, basil, fennel seed, salt, and pepper to insert and combine with turkey sausage.

3. Secure the lid and make sure the valve is pointing up to SEALING.

4. Press MANUAL (or press PRESSURE COOK and select HIGH PRESSURE) and adjust time to 5 minutes.

5. When multicooker signals the end of cooking time, press CANCEL, and then quick release the pressure by turning the valve down to VENTING with the handle of a wooden spoon or other device to prevent the steam from burning your hands during the release.

6. Remove lid and stir sauce.

7. Serve over cooked pasta and garnish with shredded Parmesan cheese.

# BALSAMIC POT ROAST WITH GRAVY

Prep time: 15 minutes | Pressurization and cooking time: 1 hour 30 minutes or more, depending on size of roast | Total time: 1 hour 45 minutes or more, depending on size of roast | Yields: 6 to 8 servings

---

| | | | |
|---|---|---|---|
| 1 | teaspoon salt | 4 | celery stalks, diced |
| 1 | teaspoon ground black pepper | 1 | (14-ounce) can low-sodium beef broth |
| 1 | teaspoon garlic powder | 1 | tablespoon Worcestershire sauce |
| 1 | (3 to 5 pound) beef chuck roast | 1 | tablespoon low-sodium soy sauce |
| 1 | tablespoon olive oil | ½ | cup balsamic vinegar |
| 1 | onion, sliced | 2 | tablespoons water |
| 1 | (16-ounce) bag baby carrots | 2 | tablespoons cornstarch |

1. In a small bowl, combine salt, pepper, and garlic powder.

2. Rub mixture over all sides of the roast and set aside.

3. Pour olive oil into the insert of a multicooker and press SAUTÉ.

4. When oil is hot and begins to ripple, sear roast on each side 2 to 3 minutes, until just starting to brown.

5. Press CANCEL and move roast, so it is in the middle of the multicooker insert.

6. Place onion slices, carrots, and celery around the edges of the roast.

7. In a small bowl, whisk together beef broth, Worcestershire sauce, soy sauce, and balsamic vinegar.

8. Pour sauce over the top of the roast and vegetables.

9. Secure the lid and make sure the valve is pointing up to SEALING.

10. Press MANUAL (or press PRESSURE COOK and select HIGH PRESSURE) and adjust time to 60 minutes for a 3-pound roast, 70 minutes for a 4-pound roast, or 80 minutes for a 5-pound roast.

11. When multicooker signals the end of cooking time, let pressure naturally release 10 minutes and then carefully turn valve to VENTING to quick release any remaining pressure.

12. Press CANCEL and then carefully transfer roast and vegetables to a serving tray and cover with foil to keep warm.

13. To make gravy, use a strainer or slotted spoon to remove any food pieces from the drippings left in the multicooker.

14. Press SAUTÉ on the multicooker.

15. In a small bowl, whisk together cornstarch and water and then whisk the mixture into the drippings in the multicooker.

16. Whisk continuously until sauce is thickened and boiling, about 2–3 minutes.

17. Slice roast and serve with vegetables and gravy.

# ITALIAN POT ROAST

Prep time: 10 minutes | Pressurization and cooking time: 1 hour 25 minutes | Total time: 1 hour 35 minutes | Yields: 6 servings

1  (3-pound) chuck roast
   Salt and pepper, to taste
1  tablespoon olive oil
1  (1-ounce) packet dry onion soup mix

1  (1-ounce) packet brown gravy mix
1  (1-ounce) packet Italian dressing mix
1½  cups beef broth

1. Season roast with salt and pepper on all sides.

2. Add olive oil to the insert of a multicooker and press SAUTÉ.

3. When oil is hot and rippling, sear roast 2 to 3 minutes on each side. When roast is browned on all sides, press CANCEL.

4. In a medium bowl, whisk together broth and all 3 mix packets. Pour broth mixture over roast.

5. Secure the lid and make sure the valve is pointing up to SEALING.

6. Press MANUAL (or press PRESSURE COOK and select HIGH PRESSURE) and adjust time to 60 minutes.

7. When multicooker signals the end of cooking time, let pressure naturally release 10 minutes and then carefully turn the valve to VENTING to quick release remaining pressure.

8. Remove lid, transfer roast to a serving platter, slice, and serve.

# FRENCH DIP SANDWICHES

Prep time: 5 minutes | Pressurization and cooking time: 1 hour 30 minutes | Total time: 1 hour 35 minutes | Yields: 8 servings

1 (3-pound) chuck roast

2 (14.5 ounce) cans beef consommé

8 sandwich rolls

1. Lightly spray the insert of a multicooker with nonstick cooking spray.

2. Place the roast in the bottom of the insert and pour the beef consommé over it.

3. Secure the lid and make sure the valve is pointing up to SEALING.

4. Press MANUAL (or press PRESSURE COOK and select HIGH PRESSURE) and adjust time to 60 minutes.

5. When multicooker signals the end of cooking time, let pressure naturally release 15 minutes then carefully turn the valve to VENTING to quick release any remaining pressure.

6. Remove lid and transfer roast to a platter; shred the beef using 2 forks.

7. Spoon juices from the insert into small bowls; serve the shredded beef on buns with the juices alongside as dipping sauce.

# BEEF AND BROCCOLI

Prep time: 10 minutes | Pressurization and cooking time: 30 minutes | Total time: 40 minutes | Yields: 6 servings

1 tablespoon olive oil

1 (1.5-pound) boneless chuck roast, cut into strips

2 teaspoons minced garlic

½ cup beef broth

½ cup low-sodium soy sauce

¼ cup brown sugar

6 to 7 cups broccoli florets, steamed to desired tenderness (see note)

1 tablespoon cornstarch

3 to 4 cups hot, cooked rice

1. Add olive oil to the insert of a multicooker and press SAUTÉ.

2. When oil is hot and rippling, add beef strips and garlic. Sauté until meat is browned, stirring frequently, about 8 minutes.

3. Add beef broth, soy sauce, and brown sugar and stir together until sugar has dissolved. Press CANCEL.

4. Secure the lid and make sure the valve is pointing up to SEALING.

5. Press MANUAL (or press PRESSURE COOK and select HIGH PRESSURE) and adjust time to 15 minutes.

6. When multicooker signals the end of cooking time, press CANCEL, and then quick release the pressure by turning the valve down to VENTING with the handle of a wooden spoon or other device to prevent the steam from burning your hands during the release.

7. Remove lid and use a ladle to scoop out ¼ cup of the liquid in the pot. Transfer liquid to a small bowl and whisk in cornstarch. Mix until smooth and then stir back into multicooker insert.

8. Press SAUTÉ and bring sauce to a simmer, stirring frequently until thickened slightly, about 5 minutes. Press CANCEL.

9. Add cooked broccoli to the pot and stir briefly to coat broccoli with the sauce. Serve immediately, over hot cooked rice.

*Note: Steam broccoli while multicooker comes to pressure and meat cooks. To easily steam, bring a large pot of water to boil. Add broccoli and cook 3 minutes. Drain off water and set broccoli aside until ready to use.*

# MEATLOAF AND MASHED POTATOES

Prep time: 15 minutes | Pressurization and cooking time: 45 minutes | Total time: 1 hour | Yields: 6 to 8

---

6 to 8  small red or Yukon Gold potatoes, peeled

1  cup water

1½  pounds ground beef

2  eggs

1  small onion, chopped

1  cup rolled oats

¼  cup ketchup

Salt and pepper, to taste

1  (10.75-ounce) can tomato soup, divided

2  tablespoons Worcestershire sauce, divided

2  tablespoons brown sugar

3  tablespoons butter

3  tablespoons milk

1. Place potatoes in an even layer in the insert of a multicooker and then place metal rack or trivet on top of potatoes. Pour water over top.

2. In a large bowl, stir together ground beef, eggs, onion, oats, ketchup, salt and pepper, ½ of the soup, and 1 tablespoon of the Worcestershire sauce.

3. Press mixture into a multicooker pan and set aside. (See note below.)

4. In a small bowl, stir together brown sugar, the remaining 1 tablespoon Worcestershire sauce, and the rest of the soup; spread evenly over top of meatloaf.

5. Place meatloaf pan on the trivet in the multicooker.

6. Secure the lid and make sure the valve is pointing up to SEALING.

7. Press MANUAL (or press PRESSURE COOK and select HIGH PRESSURE) and adjust time to 30 minutes.

8. When multicooker signals the end of cooking time, press CANCEL, and then quick release the pressure by turning the valve down to VENTING with the handle of a wooden spoon or other device to prevent the steam from burning your hands during the release.

9. Remove lid and then carefully transfer meatloaf pan from the pot to a wire rack on the counter.

10. Remove trivet from multicooker insert and then add butter and milk to the potatoes. Season with salt and pepper to taste, and then mash with a fork or potato masher to desired texture.

11. Slice meatloaf and serve with mashed potatoes.

*Note: If you do not have a multicooker pan, you can shape one out of several layers of heavy-duty aluminum foil.*

# CREAMY SHELLS AND BEEF

Prep time: 15 minutes | Pressurization and cooking time: 25 to 30 minutes | Total time: 40 to 45 minutes | Yields: 6 servings

| | |
|---|---|
| 1 tablespoon olive oil | 1 (16-ounce) package medium pasta shells |
| 1 onion, diced | 1 (24-ounce) jar pasta sauce |
| 1 pound lean ground beef | 3 cups water |
| 1 tablespoon Italian seasoning | 1 cup grated Parmesan cheese |
| 1 teaspoon garlic powder | 1 cup half and half |
| ½ teaspoon salt | 4 ounces cream cheese, softened |
| ½ teaspoon ground black pepper | Chopped fresh parsley, for garnishing |
| 1 tablespoon tomato paste | |

1. Pour olive oil in the insert of a multicooker and press SAUTÉ.

2. Add diced onion and sauté 2 to 3 minutes, until onion starts to soften.

3. Add ground beef to the pot and use a wooden spoon to break meat into small pieces. Cook until browned, about 3–5 minutes.

4. Press CANCEL and drain excess grease from insert.

5. Return insert to multicooker. Add Italian seasoning, garlic powder, salt, pepper, and tomato paste to the beef mixture; stir to combine.

6. Pour uncooked pasta shells on top of the ground beef mixture, followed by water and then pasta sauce, but DO NOT stir.

7. Secure the lid and make sure the valve is pointing up to SEALING.

8. Press MANUAL (or press PRESSURE COOK and select HIGH PRESSURE) and adjust time to 5 minutes.

9. When multicooker signals the end of cooking time, press CANCEL, and then quick release the pressure by turning the valve down to VENTING with the handle of a wooden spoon or other device to prevent the steam from burning your hands during the release.

10. Remove lid and stir in Parmesan cheese, half and half, and cream cheese. Combine well.

11. Serve, garnished with fresh parsley, if desired.

# PHILLY CHEESESTEAK SANDWICHES

Prep time: 10 minutes | Pressurization and cooking time: 33 to 35 minutes | Total time: 43 to 45 minutes | Yields: 4 servings

1 tablespoon olive oil

1 green bell pepper, sliced

1 medium onion, sliced

1 (1.5-pound) round steak, thinly sliced

1 (1-ounce) packet Italian dressing mix

1¼ cups beef broth

1 loaf French bread

8 ounces Kraft Velveeta Cheese

½ teaspoon ground black pepper

½ teaspoon salt

¼ cup milk

1. Add olive oil to the insert of a multicooker and press SAUTÉ.

2. When oil is hot and rippling, add peppers and onions and cook until onion is soft and translucent, about 5 minutes.

3. Add sliced steak and Italian dressing mix and sauté meat with vegetables 2 minutes. Pour in beef broth and stir to combine. Press CANCEL.

4. Secure the lid and make sure the valve is pointing up to SEALING.

5. Press MANUAL (or press PRESSURE COOK and select HIGH PRESSURE) and adjust time to 8 minutes.

6. When multicooker signals the end of cooking time, let pressure naturally release 10 minutes and then carefully turn the valve to VENTING to quick release remaining pressure.

7. Prepare cheese sauce: In a medium pan over medium heat, warm Velveeta, milk, salt, and pepper, stirring occasionally until cheese melts.

8. Cut French bread into 4 pieces and split each piece horizontally to make the top and bottom halves for 4 sandwiches.

9. Scoop meat onto 4 halves, spoon on some cheese sauce, and top with remaining bread halves.

# HONEY-GLAZED HAM

Prep time: 10 minutes | Pressurization and cooking time: 25 minutes | Total time: 35 minutes | Yields: 8–10 servings

| | | | |
|---|---|---|---|
| 1½ | cups water | ¼ | teaspoon ground nutmeg |
| 2 | tablespoons Dijon mustard | ½ | teaspoon ground cinnamon |
| ½ | cup brown sugar | 1 | (3- to 4-pound) boneless spiral ham |
| ½ | cup honey | | |

1. Place trivet in the insert of a multicooker and pour water in insert.

2. Prepare glaze by mixing together mustard, brown sugar, honey, nutmeg, and cinnamon in a small bowl.

3. Lay a large piece of heavy-duty aluminum foil on counter and place ham in the middle of the foil. Fold up sides of foil to make a bowl-like shape around the ham.

4. Brush ⅔ of the mixture on top of and in between slices of ham then place ham in its foil bowl on top of the trivet.

5. Secure the lid and make sure the valve is pointing up to SEALING.

6. Press MANUAL (or press PRESSURE COOK and select HIGH PRESSURE) and adjust time to 4 minutes for a 3-pound ham or 5 minutes for a 4-pound ham.

7. When multicooker signals the end of cooking time, let pressure naturally release 10 minutes and then carefully turn the valve to VENTING to quick release remaining pressure.

8. Remove the ham from the multicooker and pour remaining sauce over top. Serve warm.

# SWEET PORK

Prep time: 5 minutes | Pressurization and cooking time: 1 hour 45 minutes | Total time: 1 hour 50 minutes | Yields: 8 servings

1   (6- to 8-pound) boneless pork roast

2   cups Coca-Cola

1   cup brown sugar

1   (15-ounce) bottle mild taco sauce

1. Cut pork roast into 4 or 5 pieces and place in the insert of a multicooker.

2. Pour Coca-Cola over the roast.

3. Sprinkle brown sugar on top of roast and pour taco sauce over the top.

4. Secure the lid and make sure the valve is pointing up to SEALING.

5. Press MANUAL (or press PRESSURE COOK and select HIGH PRESSURE) and adjust time to 90 minutes.

6. When multicooker signals the end of cooking time, press CANCEL, and then quick release the pressure by turning the valve down to VENTING with the handle of a wooden spoon or other device to prevent the steam from burning your hands during the release.

7. Remove roast pieces from the multicooker and transfer to a large bowl; shred with 2 forks.

8. Transfer shredded pork back into the juices in the multicooker, stir, and then use a slotted spoon or tongs to serve on tortillas with your favorite toppings.

# PORK CARNITAS

Prep time: 20 minutes | Pressurization and cooking time: 1 hour 15 minutes | Total time: 1 hour 35 minutes | Yields: 6 to 8 servings

2    teaspoons salt

½    teaspoon ground black pepper

1    teaspoon ground cumin

½    teaspoon chili powder

½    teaspoon paprika

1    (3-pound) boneless pork shoulder or pork butt roast, cut into 2-inch cubes

1    tablespoon olive oil

1    cup orange juice

1    small onion, peeled and quartered

2    cloves garlic, minced

1. In a small bowl, stir together salt, pepper, cumin, chili powder, and paprika; set aside.

2. Place cubed roast in a large bowl and toss with olive oil. Sprinkle spice mixture over pork cubes and toss again.

3. Place pork cubes in the insert of a multicooker, followed by orange juice, onion, and minced garlic.

4. Secure the lid and make sure the valve is pointing up to SEALING.

5. Press MANUAL (or press PRESSURE COOK and select HIGH PRESSURE) and adjust time to 20 minutes.

6. When multicooker signals the end of cooking time, press CANCEL, and then quick release the pressure by turning the valve down to VENTING with the handle of a wooden spoon or other device to prevent the steam from burning your hands during the release.

7. Transfer pork to a large bowl, shred, and serve plain or as the filling in your favorite Tex-Mex dish, such as enchiladas, tacos, burritos, or salad.

# BBQ PULLED PORK SANDWICHES AND COLESLAW

Prep time: 20 minutes | Pressurization and cooking time: 1 hour 25 minutes | Total time: 1 hour 45 minutes | Yields: 8 servings

## Coleslaw

| | |
|---|---|
| 1 | (14-ounce) package coleslaw mix |
| 1 | cup Light Miracle Whip |
| 2 | tablespoons white vinegar |

| | |
|---|---|
| 1 | teaspoon granulated sugar |
| ¼ | teaspoon onion powder |
| | Salt and pepper, to taste |

## Pulled Pork Sandwiches

| | |
|---|---|
| 1 | (4-pound) boneless pork shoulder roast |
| ½ | cup BBQ seasoning, such as Traeger Grill Seasoning and BBQ Rub |
| 1 | tablespoon olive oil |
| 1 | (14-ounce) can beef broth |
| 3 | tablespoons Worcestershire sauce |

| | |
|---|---|
| ½ | teaspoon liquid smoke |
| | Salt and pepper, to taste |
| 1 | (18-ounce) bottle BBQ sauce |
| 8 | hamburger buns |

1. Prepare coleslaw: In a large bowl, toss together coleslaw mix, Miracle Whip, vinegar, sugar, and onion powder. Season with salt and pepper, to taste. Cover and store in refrigerator until just before serving.

2. Cut pork roast into 4 pieces and rub BBQ seasoning on all sides of each piece; set aside.

3. Pour olive oil in the insert of a multicooker, press SAUTÉ, and heat oil until it ripples.

4. Sear the 4 pieces of pork roast on each side, 2 to 3 minutes, until just starting to brown.

5. Press CANCEL and transfer pork to a plate or bowl and set aside.

6. Pour beef broth, Worcestershire sauce, and liquid smoke into the insert and use a spatula or wooden spoon to deglaze the pot and release any bits of cooked meat from the bottom of the pot.

7. Return pork to the insert and season with salt and pepper, to taste.

8. Secure the lid and make sure the valve is pointing up to SEALING.

9. Press MANUAL (or press PRESSURE COOK and select HIGH PRESSURE) and adjust time to 60 minutes.

10. When multicooker signals the end of cooking time, let pressure naturally release 10 minutes and then carefully turn the valve to VENTING to quick release remaining pressure.

11. Remove pork from the multicooker, place in a bowl, and shred using two forks.

12. Mix in BBQ sauce until well combined.

13. Spoon shredded pork onto bottom half of each bun; top with coleslaw and top half of bun.

# BBQ COUNTRY RIBS

Prep time: 10 minutes | Pressurization and cooking time: 45 to 50 minutes | Total time: 55 to 60 minutes | Yields: 6 to 8 servings

---

3 to 4 pounds boneless, country style pork ribs

⅓ cup BBQ seasoning, such as Traeger Grill Seasoning and BBQ Rub

1½ cups apple juice

1 tablespoon liquid smoke

¼ cup apple cider vinegar

1 cup BBQ sauce

1. Rub all sides of the ribs with BBQ seasoning; set aside.

2. Pour apple juice, liquid smoke, and vinegar in the insert of a multicooker and place trivet in the bottom of the insert.

3. Place ribs on the trivet, being careful not to overlap too much.

4. Secure the lid and make sure the valve is pointing up to SEALING.

5. Press MANUAL (or press PRESSURE COOK and select HIGH PRESSURE) and adjust time to 25 minutes.

6. When multicooker signals the end of cooking time, let pressure naturally release 10 minutes and then carefully turn the valve to VENTING to quick release remaining pressure.

7. Preheat oven broiler to low; line a baking sheet with aluminum foil.

8. Using tongs, remove ribs from the multicooker insert and place on prepared baking sheet.

9. Spread BBQ sauce on top of ribs and place under broiler until sauce begins to caramelize, about 1–2 minutes. Watch closely to avoid burning or drying out ribs.

10. Remove from oven and serve.

# BONE-IN RIBS

Prep time: 5 minutes | Pressurization and cooking time: 50 minutes | Total time: 55 minutes | Yields: 5 servings

| | | | |
|---|---|---|---|
| 1 | (2- to 3-pound) rack pork ribs | 3½ | cups apple juice, divided |
| 1 | teaspoon salt | 1½ | cups brown sugar, divided |
| 1 | teaspoon ground black pepper | 1 | (16-ounce) bottle BBQ sauce |

1. Season ribs with salt and pepper on both sides. Place trivet in the insert of a multicooker, then place ribs on top of trivet. Cut ribs into smaller sections if they don't fit well in the insert.

2. In a medium bowl, whisk together 3¼ cups of the apple juice and the brown sugar and then pour over ribs.

3. Secure the lid and make sure the valve is pointing up to SEALING.

4. Press MANUAL (or press PRESSURE COOK and select HIGH PRESSURE) and adjust time to 30 minutes.

5. When multicooker signals the end of cooking time, let pressure naturally release until steam is completely dispersed.

6. Preheat oven broiler to high and line a baking sheet with foil.

7. Carefully remove multicooker lid and transfer ribs to a foil-lined baking sheet; set aside.

8. In a medium bowl, whisk together remaining ¼ cup apple juice and the bottle of BBQ sauce. Brush ribs generously with sauce and place under the broiler.

9. Broil 2 to 3 minutes then flip ribs and slather with more sauce. Repeat one more time. Sauce will begin to turn sticky when ribs are done.

# HONEY-SOY PORK CHOPS

Prep time: 5 minutes | Pressurization and cooking time: 25 minutes | Total time: 30 minutes | Yields: 4 servings

⅓   cup soy sauce

½   cup plus 2 teaspoons water, divided

½   cup honey

1   tablespoon fresh ginger

1   teaspoon minced garlic

1   tablespoon sesame oil

4   boneless pork chops

2   teaspoons cornstarch

4   green onions, chopped, for garnishing

1   teaspoon sesame seeds, for garnishing

1. In the insert of a multicooker, combine soy sauce, ½ cup water, honey, ginger, garlic, and sesame oil. Place pork chops in mixture.

2. Secure the lid and make sure the valve is pointing up to SEALING.

3. Press MANUAL (or press PRESSURE COOK and select HIGH PRESSURE) and adjust time to 6 minutes.

4. When multicooker signals the end of cooking time, let pressure naturally release 10 minutes.

5. Press CANCEL, remove lid, and transfer pork chops to a plate. Leave the insert with liquid in it in the multicooker.

6. In a small bowl, combine cornstarch with remaining 2 teaspoons water and mix well.

7. Press SAUTÉ on the multicooker and pour cornstarch mixture into hot liquid. Stir until thickened and bubbly, about 2–3 minutes.

8. Pour sauce over the pork chops and serve garnished with sliced green onions and sesame seeds.

# SOUR CREAM PORK CHOPS

Prep time: 10 minutes | Pressurization and cooking time: 20 to 25 minutes | Total time: 30 to 35 minutes | Yields: 4 servings

---

| | | | |
|---|---|---|---|
| 4 | pork chops | 1 | cup beef broth |
| | Salt and pepper, to taste | 1 | tablespoon Worcestershire sauce |
| 1 | tablespoon butter | 1 | teaspoon cornstarch |
| 1 | sweet onion, diced | ½ | cup sour cream |

1. Season both sides of pork chops with salt and pepper and set aside.

2. Add butter to the insert of a multicooker and press SAUTÉ.

3. When butter is melted, add onions and sauté until softened, about 5 minutes.

4. With a slotted spoon, remove onions from the insert and set aside in a small bowl. Add seasoned pork chops to the bottom of the insert and brown 1 minute on each side.

5. Press CANCEL and transfer pork chops to a plate.

6. Pour beef broth in insert and use a spatula to deglaze the bottom of the pot, scraping up all the browned bits.

7. Stir in Worcestershire sauce and then return onions and pork chops to the pot.

8. Secure the lid and make sure the valve is pointing up to SEALING.

9. Press MANUAL (or press PRESSURE COOK and select HIGH PRESSURE) and adjust time to 8 minutes.

10. When multicooker signals the end of cooking time, let pressure naturally release 5 minutes, then carefully turn valve to VENTING to quick release remaining pressure.

11. Remove pork chops from the liquid and set aside on a plate or serving platter.

12. Whisk cornstarch into the liquid in the pot and stir until slightly thickened, about 1 to 2 minutes. Add sour cream and stir until combined.

13. To serve, pour sour cream mixture over pork chops like a gravy.

# ITALIAN SAUSAGE SPAGHETTI

Prep time: 15 minutes | Pressurization and cooking time: 22 to 25 minutes | Total time: 37 to 40 minutes | Yields: 4 to 6 servings

| | | | |
|---|---|---|---|
| 1 | pound mild ground Italian sausage | 2 | cups water |
| 1 | teaspoon Italian seasoning | 8 | ounces uncooked spaghetti |
| ½ | teaspoon garlic powder | 1 | (24-ounce) jar marinara sauce |
| | Salt and pepper, to taste | | Shredded parmesan cheese, for topping |

1. Press SAUTÉ to heat multicooker insert; add sausage and use a wooden spoon to break up meat and cook until browned, about 7 to 10 minutes.

2. Press CANCEL and then add the Italian seasoning, garlic powder, salt, pepper, and water. Mix until well combined, scraping up any browned bits from the bottom of the pot.

3. Break the spaghetti noodles in half and layer in different directions on top of sauce.

4. Pour marinara sauce over spaghetti, but DO NOT stir the sauce into the water. Try to cover all the noodles with the marinara sauce.

5. Secure the lid and make sure the valve is pointing up to SEALING.

6. Press MANUAL (or press PRESSURE COOK and select HIGH PRESSURE) and adjust time to 8 minutes.

7. When multicooker signals the end of cooking time, press CANCEL, and then quick release the pressure by turning the valve down to VENTING with the handle of a wooden spoon or other device to prevent the steam from burning your hands during the release.

8. Stir spaghetti, sauce, and sausage until combined and let sit 3 to 5 minutes before serving to absorb excess liquid.

9. Serve, topped with shredded parmesan cheese.

# EGG ROLLS IN A BOWL

Prep time: 8 to 10 minutes | Pressurization and cooking time: 10 to 15 minutes | Total time: 18 to 25 minutes | Yields: 4 to 6 servings

1   **pound ground pork**

1   **tablespoon soy sauce**

1   **tablespoon garlic powder**

1   **tablespoon ground ginger**

½   **teaspoon ground black pepper**

½   **teaspoon salt**

½   **cup chicken broth**

1   **bag coleslaw mix**

     **Teriyaki sauce, for drizzling on top**

1. Press SAUTÉ to heat multicooker insert; add sausage and use a wooden spoon to start breaking up meat. Add soy sauce, garlic powder, ginger, pepper, and salt. Stir seasonings into meat and cook meat until it is browned and no more pink remains, about 8 minutes. Drain off any excess grease.

2. Press CANCEL, and then add chicken broth and coleslaw mix but DO NOT stir.

3. Secure the lid and make sure the valve is pointing up to SEALING.

4. Press MANUAL (or press PRESSURE COOK and select HIGH PRESSURE) and adjust time to 0 minutes.

5. When multicooker signals the end of cooking time, press CANCEL, and then quick release the pressure by turning the valve down to VENTING with the handle of a wooden spoon or other device to prevent the steam from burning your hands during the release.

6. Remove lid, stir mixture, then dish into bowls to serve. Drizzle with teriyaki sauce, if desired.

# HAWAIIAN MEATBALLS

Prep time: 5 minutes | Pressurization and cooking time: 17 minutes | Total time: 22 minutes | Yields: 6 servings

1 (32-ounce) package precooked frozen meatballs

1 (20-ounce) can pineapple chunks, undrained

1 red bell pepper, diced

1 cup brown sugar

⅔ cup white vinegar

2 tablespoons soy sauce

3 to 4 cups hot, cooked rice

1. Place meatballs in the bottom of the multicooker insert.

2. Top with pineapple chunks and red pepper.

3. Spoon brown sugar, vinegar, and soy sauce over the top but do not stir.

4. Secure the lid and make sure the valve is pointing up to SEALING.

5. Press MANUAL (or press PRESSURE COOK and select HIGH PRESSURE) and adjust time to 7 minutes.

6. When multicooker signals the end of cooking time, press CANCEL, and then quick release the pressure by turning the valve down to VENTING with the handle of a wooden spoon or other device to prevent the steam from burning your hands during the release.

7. Remove the lid and stir to coat meatballs and pineapple with sauce.

8. Serve over hot, cooked rice.

# BISCUITS AND GRAVY

Prep time: 10 minutes | Pressurization and cooking time: 15 minutes | Total time: 25 minutes | Yields: 6 to 8 servings

| | | | |
|---|---|---|---|
| 1 | pound ground sausage | ½ | teaspoon salt |
| ½ | cup chicken broth | ½ | teaspoon ground black pepper |
| ½ | cup all-purpose flour | 6 to 8 | freshly baked biscuits, canned or homemade |
| 3 | cups milk | | |

1. Press SAUTÉ to heat multicooker insert; add sausage and use a wooden spoon to break up meat and cook until browned, about 5 to 7 minutes.

2. Press CANCEL and add chicken broth.

3. Secure the lid and make sure the valve is pointing up to SEALING.

4. Press MANUAL (or press PRESSURE COOK and select HIGH PRESSURE) and adjust time to 5 minutes.

5. While multicooker pressurizes and sausage mixture cooks, whisk together flour and milk in a medium bowl.

6. When multicooker signals the end of cooking time, press CANCEL, and then quick release the pressure by turning the valve down to VENTING with the handle of a wooden spoon or other device to prevent the steam from burning your hands during the release.

7. Remove lid and press SAUTÉ. Stir in the milk-flour mixture then add salt and pepper.

8. Stir until the gravy becomes thick and bubbly, about 5 minutes.

9. Serve over freshly made biscuits.

# BREAKFAST HASH

Prep time: 10 minutes | Pressurization and cooking time: 25 minutes | Total time: 35 minutes | Yields: 4 servings

| | | | |
|---|---|---|---|
| 1 | tablespoon olive oil | ¼ | teaspoon paprika |
| ½ | pound bacon, chopped | | Salt and pepper, to taste |
| ½ | yellow onion, diced | 1 | pound baby yellow potatoes, halved |
| 1 | red bell pepper, diced | ⅔ | cup chicken broth |
| 1 | green bell pepper, diced | 4 | eggs, fried over easy or sunny side up, for topping |
| 2 | teaspoons minced garlic | | Fresh chopped parsley, for garnishing |
| ½ | teaspoon ground cumin | | |

1. Add olive oil to the insert of a multicooker and press SAUTÉ.

2. When oil is hot and rippling, add bacon, onion, and peppers to the insert and sauté until vegetables are tender and bacon is cooked, about 5 to 7 minutes.

3. Add garlic, cumin, paprika, salt, and pepper and stir until combined and fragrant, about 1 minute; press CANCEL.

4. Add potatoes to the insert and pour chicken broth over top.

5. Secure the lid and make sure the valve is pointing up to SEALING.

6. Press MANUAL (or press PRESSURE COOK and select HIGH PRESSURE) and adjust time to 9 minutes.

7. When the multicooker is about halfway finished counting down, prepare eggs to your liking—sunny side up or over easy.

8. When multicooker signals the end of cooking time, press CANCEL, and then quick release the pressure by turning the valve down to VENTING with the handle of a wooden spoon or other device to prevent the steam from burning your hands during the release.

9. Remove lid and stir.

10. Using a slotted spoon, portion potatoes, peppers, and onions into bowls.

11. Top each bowl with a fried egg and a sprinkle of fresh parsley.

# SALMON AND POTATOES

Prep time: 5 minutes | Pressurization and cooking time: 13 minutes | Total time: 18 minutes | Yields: 4 servings

---

1 pound baby potatoes

1 cup water

2 tablespoons butter

Garlic salt, to taste

Ground black pepper, to taste

1 (1-pound) salmon fillet, about 1-inch thick

Zest and juice from 1 lemon

Paprika, to taste

1. Place potatoes in the insert of a multicooker.

2. Cover potatoes with 1 cup of water, then add butter, garlic salt, and pepper to the mix and place the steamer rack over the top. Place a layer of foil on the steamer rack.

3. Place salmon, skin-side down, on the foil. Sprinkle with lemon zest, paprika, and more garlic salt; pour lemon juice over the top.

4. Secure the lid and make sure the valve is pointing up to SEALING.

5. Press MANUAL (or press PRESSURE COOK and select HIGH PRESSURE) and adjust time to 3 minutes.

6. When multicooker signals the end of cooking time, press CANCEL, and then quick release the pressure by turning the valve down to VENTING with the handle of a wooden spoon or other device to prevent the steam from burning your hands during the release.

7. Carefully remove the lid and transfer salmon to a serving platter. Scoop out baby potatoes and serve on the side.

# TERIYAKI PINEAPPLE SALMON

Prep time: 5 minutes | Pressurization and cooking time: 25 minutes | Total time: 30 minutes | Yields: 4 servings

1   cup water

4   (2.5-ounce) salmon filets

⅓   cup teriyaki sauce, divided

4   pineapple rings, canned

2   tablespoons pineapple juice, reserved from canned pineapple slices

1   teaspoon chopped cilantro

1. Pour 1 cup water in the insert of a multicooker and place a trivet in the pot.

2. Spray a 7-inch cake pan or springform pan with nonstick cooking spray and set pan on top of trivet.

3. Arrange salmon filets in the cake pan and baste filets with half of the teriyaki sauce. Place a pineapple ring over each glazed filet.

4. Secure the lid and make sure the valve is pointing up to SEALING.

5. Press MANUAL (or press PRESSURE COOK and select HIGH PRESSURE) and adjust time to 3 minutes.

6. When multicooker signals the end of cooking time, press CANCEL, and then quick release the pressure by turning the valve down to VENTING with the handle of a wooden spoon or other device to prevent the steam from burning your hands during the release.

7. Press CANCEL and remove the pan and trivet from the insert and set aside. Transfer salmon and pineapple rings to a plate or serving platter. Empty any remaining water from the insert and return insert to multicooker.

8. Press SAUTÉ and add pineapple juice and remaining teriyaki sauce to the insert. Whisk until the sauce thickens, about 5 minutes.

9. To serve, plate each salmon filet and top with a pineapple ring and a generous spoonful of sauce. Garnish with a sprinkle of chopped cilantro.

# CREAMY COCONUT SHRIMP

Prep time: 5 minutes | Pressurization and cooking time: 15 to 20 minutes | Total time: 20 to 25 minutes | Yields: 4 servings

| | |
|---|---|
| 1 tablespoon coconut oil | 1 tablespoon granulated sugar |
| 2 tablespoons minced garlic | ¼ teaspoon salt |
| 2 pounds large shrimp, peeled and deveined | ⅛ teaspoon ground black pepper |
| ½ cup coconut milk | 1 (2.25-ounce) package chopped walnuts for garnish (optional) |
| ¼ cup 2 percent milk | 4 cups hot, cooked rice |

1. Add coconut oil to the insert of a multicooker and press SAUTÉ.

2. When oil is hot and rippling, add garlic and sauté until garlic is fragrant, about 30 seconds. Add shrimp and sauté 2 minutes. Press CANCEL.

3. Pour in coconut milk and 2 percent milk and use a rubber spatula to deglaze the bottom of the insert by scraping up any browned bits.

4. Add sugar, salt, and pepper, and stir to mix all ingredients.

5. Secure the lid and make sure the valve is pointing up to SEALING.

6. Press MANUAL (or press PRESSURE COOK and select HIGH PRESSURE) and adjust time to 5 minutes.

7. When multicooker signals the end of cooking time, press CANCEL, and then quick release the pressure by turning the valve down to VENTING with the handle of a wooden spoon or other device to prevent the steam from burning your hands during the release.

8. Remove lid and transfer shrimp and sauce to a serving bowl. Top with walnuts, if desired, and serve over hot, cooked rice.

# CAJUN SHRIMP AND SAUSAGE

Prep time: 10 minutes | Pressurization and cooking time: 15–20 minutes | Total time: 25–30 minutes | Yields: 4 servings

| | | | |
|---|---|---|---|
| 2 | tablespoons butter | ½ | teaspoon dried oregano |
| 1 | teaspoon minced garlic | 1 | (10-ounce) package fettuccine |
| 1 | pound cooked shrimp | 3 | cups chicken broth |
| 1 | (1-pound) package andouille sausage, sliced | 1 | cup heavy cream |
| 1 | teaspoon cajun seasoning | 1 | cup shredded parmesan cheese |

1. Add butter, garlic, shrimp, sausage, cajun seasoning, and dried oregano to the insert of a multicooker and press SAUTÉ.

2. Sauté until sausage begins to brown on the outside edges (about 3–4 minutes).

3. Press CANCEL. Scrape the bottom of the insert.

4. Add fettucine and broth, making sure all the noodles are covered in liquid.

5. Secure the lid and make sure the valve is pointing up to SEALING.

6. Press MANUAL (or press PRESSURE COOK and select HIGH PRESSURE) and adjust time to 5 minutes.

7. When multicooker signals the end of cooking time, press CANCEL, and then quick release the pressure by turning the valve down to VENTING with the handle of a wooden spoon or other device to prevent the steam from burning your hands during the release.

8. Remove lid and stir in heavy cream and parmesan cheese until the cheese has completely melted. Season to taste with more cajun seasoning.

# CREAMY SHRIMP ALFREDO

Prep time: 10 minutes | Pressurization and cooking time: 35 minutes | Total time: 45 minutes | Yields: 4 to 6 servings

| | | | |
|---|---|---|---|
| 12 | ounces fettuccine or penne pasta | 2 | tablespoons butter |
| 3 | cups water | 1 | clove garlic, minced |
| 1 | pound shrimp, peeled and deveined | ⅓ | cup chicken broth |
| | Salt and pepper, to taste | 2 | cups heavy cream |
| | Dash paprika | ½ | cup shredded Parmesan cheese |
| 1 | tablespoon olive oil | | Chopped fresh parsley or basil, for garnishing |
| 1 | small onion, finely chopped | | |

1. If using fettuccine noodles, break them in half. Place noodles and water in the insert of a multicooker and mix to cover noodles with water.

2. Secure the lid and make sure the valve is pointing up to SEALING.

3. Press MANUAL (or press PRESSURE COOK and select HIGH PRESSURE) and adjust time to 4 minutes.

4. When multicooker signals the end of cooking time, press CANCEL, and then quick release the pressure by turning the valve down to VENTING with the handle of a wooden spoon or other device to prevent the steam from burning your hands during the release.

5. Remove lid and transfer cooked noodles to a large bowl; set aside.

6. Season shrimp with salt, pepper, and paprika.

7. Add olive oil to multicooker insert and press SAUTÉ.

8. When oil is hot and rippling, add shrimp and cook 1 to 2 minutes on each side, until shrimp is pink and not translucent. Transfer shrimp to the bowl with noodles and set aside.

9. Melt butter in insert; add onion and garlic and sauté until the onion begins to turn golden brown, about 8 minutes.

10. Stir in chicken broth, being sure to scrape the bottom of the insert with a rubber spatula to deglaze pot.

11. Stir in cream and simmer 2 minutes, stirring often. Add Parmesan cheese and stir until creamy and smooth. Press CANCEL.

12. Stir in shrimp and pasta and adjust seasonings (salt, pepper, paprika) to taste.

13. Serve warm, garnished with fresh chopped parsley or basil.

# LOBSTER MAC AND CHEESE

Prep time: 10 minutes | Pressurization and cooking time: 15 to 18 minutes | Total time: 25 to 28 minutes | Yields: 4 servings

| | | | | |
|---|---|---|---|---|
| 12 | ounces uncooked elbow macaroni | ½ | pound cooked lobster meat |
| 3 | cups chicken broth | ½ | cup milk |
| ½ | teaspoon onion powder | ½ | cup shredded mozzarella cheese |
| 1 | tablespoon hot sauce | ½ | cup shredded cheddar cheese |
| 2 | tablespoons butter | ½ | cup shredded pepper Jack cheese |
| 1 | teaspoon minced garlic | | |

1. Place macaroni, chicken broth, onion powder, and hot sauce in the insert of a multicooker.

2. Secure the lid and make sure the valve is pointing up to SEALING.

3. Press MANUAL (or press PRESSURE COOK and select HIGH PRESSURE) and adjust time to 5 minutes.

4. After multicooker comes to pressure and the time starts to count down, melt butter in a large skillet over medium heat. Add garlic and lobster meat and sauté 2 to 3 minutes until garlic is fragrant and lobster meat is warmed through. Set aside.

5. When multicooker signals the end of cooking time, press CANCEL, and then quick release the pressure by turning the valve down to VENTING with the handle of a wooden spoon or other device to prevent the steam from burning your hands during the release.

6. Remove lid, add milk and cheeses, and stir until cheese is melted. Stir in lobster, then season with salt and pepper to taste. Serve immediately.

# LOADED MAC AND CHEESE

Prep time: 15 minutes | Pressurization and cooking time: 15 to 20 minutes | Total time: 30 to 35 minutes | Yields: 6 to 8 servings

| | | | | |
|---|---|---|---|---|
| 2½ | cups uncooked elbow macaroni | | 3 | tablespoons butter, divided |
| 3 | cups water | | ½ | cup milk |
| ½ | teaspoon onion powder | | 3 | cups shredded cheddar cheese |
| 1 | teaspoon dry mustard | | ½ | cup panko breadcrumbs |
| ¼ | teaspoon seasoning salt | | ¼ | cup minced chives |
| ¼ | teaspoon ground black pepper | | 6 | strips bacon, cooked and crumbled |
| 4 | ounces cream cheese | | | |

1. Add uncooked macaroni, water, onion powder, dry mustard, seasoning salt, and pepper to the insert of a multicooker.

2. Secure the lid and make sure the valve is pointing up to SEALING.

3. Press MANUAL (or press PRESSURE COOK and select HIGH PRESSURE) and adjust time to 5 minutes.

4. When multicooker signals the end of cooking time, quick release the pressure by turning the valve down to VENTING with the handle of a wooden spoon or other device to prevent the steam from burning your hands during the release.

5. Remove lid and add cream cheese and 1 tablespoon of the butter to the macaroni and remaining water. Stir until combined.

6. Add milk and shredded cheese and stir until cheese is melted and everything is well combined.

7. Spread macaroni mixture in an 8x10-inch serving dish and set aside.

8. Prepare a crumb topping by adding remaining 2 tablespoons butter to a medium skillet and melting over medium-high heat. Add breadcrumbs and cook, stirring constantly, until breadcrumbs are golden brown, about 2 to 3 minutes. Remove from heat and sprinkle on top of macaroni.

9. Sprinkle chives and bacon crumbles on top of toasted breadcrumbs and serve.

# CHEESY PENNE PASTA

Prep time: 10 minutes | Pressurization and cooking time: 25 minutes | Total time: 35 minutes | Yields: 6 servings

4 cups chicken broth

2 cloves garlic, minced

Salt and pepper, to taste

16 ounces dry penne pasta

1 (12-ounce) can evaporated milk

2 cups marinara sauce

1 cup shredded Parmesan cheese, plus more for garnishing

½ cup shredded mozzarella cheese

Fresh chopped basil, for garnishing (optional)

1. Add chicken broth, garlic, salt, pepper, and penne pasta to the insert of a multicooker.

2. Secure the lid and make sure the valve is pointing up to SEALING.

3. Press MANUAL (or press PRESSURE COOK and select HIGH PRESSURE) and adjust time to 5 minutes.

4. When multicooker signals the end of cooking time, let pressure naturally release 5 minutes and then carefully turn the valve to VENTING to quick release remaining pressure.

5. Remove lid and pour in evaporated milk and marinara sauce. Stir the sauce in with the pasta so that all the pasta is evenly covered. Add Parmesan cheese and mozzarella cheese and stir until cheese melts.

6. Serve immediately, topped with fresh chopped basil and shredded Parmesan cheese, if desired.

# MUSHROOM STROGANOFF

Prep time: 5 minutes | Pressurization and cooking time: 15 minutes | Total time: 20 minutes | Yields: 4 servings

| | | | |
|---|---|---|---|
| 1 | tablespoon olive oil | 2 | cups beef broth |
| 1 | sweet onion, diced | 8 | ounces wide egg noodles |
| 2 | teaspoons minced garlic | ½ | cup sour cream |
| 8 | ounces fresh white mushrooms, sliced | 2 | tablespoons fresh chopped parsley |
| 2 | (10.5-ounce) cans cream of mushroom soup | | |

1. Add olive oil to the insert of a multicooker and press SAUTÉ.

2. When oil is hot and rippling, add onion, minced garlic, and mushrooms to the insert. Sauté until the onions soften and the mushrooms begin to sweat, about 7 minutes.

3. Press CANCEL and then add cream of mushroom soup, beef broth, and wide egg noodles. Stir until noodles are almost completely covered by the sauce.

4. Secure the lid and make sure the valve is pointing up to SEALING.

5. Press MANUAL (or press PRESSURE COOK and select HIGH PRESSURE) and adjust time to 3 minutes.

6. When multicooker signals the end of cooking time, press CANCEL, and then quick release the pressure by turning the valve down to VENTING with the handle of a wooden spoon or other device to prevent the steam from burning your hands during the release.

7. Remove the lid and stir carefully before adding sour cream and mixing thoroughly.

8. Serve, garnish with fresh parsley if desired.

# VEGGIE LO MEIN

Prep time: 5 minutes | Pressurization and cooking time: 15 minutes | Total time: 20 minutes | Yields: 4 servings

---

8   ounces spaghetti noodles, broken in half

2   cups vegetable broth

1   teaspoon sesame oil

1   teaspoon minced garlic

1   tablespoon soy sauce

1   tablespoon brown sugar

1   teaspoon sriracha

1   cup sugar snap peas

1   cup carrots, sliced thin

1   red pepper, sliced thin

1   celery stalk, sliced thin

    Sliced green onions, for garnishing

    Sesame seeds, for garnishing

1. Add noodles to the insert of a multicooker.

2. In a medium bowl, mix together vegetable broth, sesame oil, garlic, soy sauce, brown sugar, and sriracha. Taste and adjust flavors as needed.

3. Pour the broth mixture over the noodles; then add peas, carrots, peppers, and celery to the insert.

4. Secure the lid and make sure the valve is pointing up to SEALING.

5. Press MANUAL (or press PRESSURE COOK and select HIGH PRESSURE) and adjust time to 4 minutes.

6. When multicooker signals the end of cooking time, press CANCEL, and then quick release the pressure by turning the valve down to VENTING with the handle of a wooden spoon or other device to prevent the steam from burning your hands during the release.

7. Remove the lid and stir the noodles.

8. Portion noodles into bowls and top with sliced green onions and sesame seeds, if desired.

# MUSHROOM RISOTTO

Prep time: 10 minutes | Pressurization and cooking time: 20 to 25 minutes | Total time: 30 to 35 minutes | Yields: 4 to 6 servings

¼  cup butter

1  medium onion, diced

2  teaspoons garlic, minced

3  cups diced mushrooms

2  cups arborio rice

4  cups chicken broth

½  teaspoon dried rosemary

Salt and pepper, to taste

½  cup grated Parmesan cheese, plus more for garnishing

Chopped fresh parsley, for garnishing

1. Add butter to the insert of a multicooker and press SAUTÉ. When butter has melted, add onion and garlic and sauté until onions are translucent, about 4 to 5 minutes. Add mushrooms to the insert and continue sautéing until mushrooms begin to brown, about 2 to 3 minutes. Press CANCEL.

2. Add rice, chicken broth, rosemary, and salt and pepper to the insert and stir briefly.

3. Secure the lid and make sure the valve is pointing up to SEALING.

4. Press MANUAL (or press PRESSURE COOK and select HIGH PRESSURE) and adjust time to 6 minutes.

5. When multicooker signals the end of cooking time, press CANCEL, and then quick release the pressure by turning the valve down to VENTING with the handle of a wooden spoon or other device to prevent the steam from burning your hands during the release.

6. Remove lid and stir in Parmesan cheese. (Any liquid remaining on top will quickly evaporate.) Serve topped with parsley and extra Parmesan cheese, if desired.

# VEGGIE FRITTATA

Prep time: 10 minutes | Pressurization and cooking time: 30 minutes | Total time: 40 minutes | Yields: 4 servings

| | | | |
|---|---|---|---|
| 6 | eggs | 1 | red pepper, diced |
| 1 | teaspoon salt | 3 to 4 | cremini mushrooms, diced |
| | Pepper, to taste | ½ | cup shredded cheddar cheese |
| 1 | cup chopped fresh spinach | 1 | cup water |

1. In a large bowl, whisk together eggs, salt, and pepper. Fold in veggies and cheese and set aside.

2. Spray a 7-inch cake pan or springform pan with nonstick cooking spray. Pour egg mixture into prepared pan and cover pan tightly with foil.

3. Pour 1 cup water into the insert of a multicooker and place trivet in the bottom of the insert. Place egg-filled pan on top of the trivet.

4. Secure the lid and make sure the valve is pointing up to SEALING.

5. Press MANUAL (or press PRESSURE COOK and select HIGH PRESSURE) and adjust time to 10 minutes.

6. When multicooker signals the end of cooking time, let pressure naturally release 10 minutes and then carefully turn the valve to VENTING to quick release remaining pressure.

7. Remove lid and transfer pan from the multicooker insert to the countertop. Remove foil, slice, and serve. (Don't worry if there is a small amount of liquid on the top of the frittata; it will evaporate).

# THREE-BEAN ENCHILADA CASSEROLE

Prep time: 10 minutes | Pressurization and cooking time: 20 minutes | Total time: 30 minutes | Yields: 6 servings

1 tablespoon olive oil

1 red bell pepper, diced

1 green bell pepper, diced

1 yellow onion, diced

2 cups green enchilada sauce, divided

1 tablespoon taco seasoning

½ cup water

1 medium zucchini, chopped

1 (15-ounce) can black beans, drained and rinsed

1 (15-ounce) can white beans, drained and rinsed

1 (15-ounce) can pinto beans, drained and rinsed

1 (15-ounce) can corn

¼ cup chopped cilantro

1 cup shredded Colby Jack cheese

2 flour tortillas, cut into thin strips

1. Add olive oil to the insert of a multicooker and press SAUTÉ.

2. When oil is hot and rippling, add diced peppers and yellow onion and cook until soft, about 5 minutes.

3. Press CANCEL and add the enchilada sauce, the taco seasoning, water, and zucchini, but DO NOT stir.

4. Secure the lid and make sure the valve is pointing up to SEALING.

5. Press MANUAL (or press PRESSURE COOK and select HIGH PRESSURE) and adjust time to 4 minutes.

6. When multicooker signals the end of cooking time, press CANCEL, and then quick release the pressure by turning the valve down to VENTING with the handle of a wooden spoon or other device to prevent the steam from burning your hands during the release.

7. Remove the lid and add the black beans, white beans, pinto beans, and corn. Stir until well combined. Add chopped cilantro and cheese and fold until well combined.

8. Sprinkle tortilla chips on top and serve with your favorite enchilada toppings, as desired.

# HEARTY BEEF STEW

Prep time: 10 minutes | Pressurization and cooking time: 55 minutes | Total time: 1 hour 5 minutes | Yields: 6 to 8 servings

1  (16-ounce) package baby carrots

3  russet potatoes, peeled and diced

2  pounds beef stew meat

2  cups beef broth

1  teaspoon Worcestershire sauce

1  tablespoon salt

½  teaspoon ground black pepper

1  onion, diced

3  celery stalks, diced

1  cup frozen green peas

1. Place all ingredients except frozen peas in the insert of a multicooker and gently stir to incorporate salt and pepper.

2. Secure the lid and make sure the valve is pointing up to SEALING.

3. Press MANUAL (or press PRESSURE COOK and select HIGH PRESSURE) and adjust time to 30 minutes.

4. When multicooker signals the end of cooking time, let pressure naturally release 10 minutes and then carefully turn the valve to VENTING to quick release remaining pressure.

5. Add frozen peas, stir until peas are well incorporated and have warmed (about 2 minutes), then serve immediately.

# CHICKEN NOODLE SOUP

Prep time: 10 minutes | Pressurization and cooking time: 20 minutes | Total time: 30 minutes | Yields: 6 servings

6   cups chicken broth

½   cup chopped onion

3   stalks celery, diced

4   large carrots, sliced

½   cup sliced green onions

1   (15-ounce) can corn, drained

½   teaspoon garlic powder

    Salt and pepper, to taste

2   cups egg noodles, uncooked

2   cups diced or shredded cooked chicken

1. Place all of the ingredients in the insert of a multicooker and stir gently so that all of the noodles are covered in the broth.

2. Secure the lid and make sure the valve is pointing up to SEALING.

3. Press MANUAL (or press PRESSURE COOK and select HIGH PRESSURE) and adjust time to 5 minutes.

4. When multicooker signals the end of cooking time, press CANCEL, and then quick release the pressure by turning the valve down to VENTING with the handle of a wooden spoon or other device to prevent the steam from burning your hands during the release.

5. Remove the lid, stir the soup, and serve.

# DUMP-AND-GO CHILI

Prep time: 10 minutes | Pressurization and cooking time: 20 minutes | Total time: 40 minutes | Yields: 6 to 8 servings

| | |
|---|---|
| 1 pound ground beef | 1 (1.25-ounce) packet chili seasoning mix |
| 1 onion, diced | 3 stalks celery, chopped |
| 2 (14-ounce) cans diced tomatoes, undrained | 2 tablespoons Worcestershire sauce |
| 1 (8-ounce) can tomato sauce | 1 tablespoon sugar |
| ⅓ cup ketchup | 1½ cups shredded cheddar cheese (optional) |
| ½ cup water | 1 (9.25-ounce) bag Fritos Corn Chips (optional) |
| 1 (15-ounce) can dark red kidney beans, drained and rinsed | |

1. Press SAUTÉ and add the ground beef and chopped onion to the insert of a multicooker. Break up ground beef with a wooden spoon and cook until beef is no longer pink, and onions are softened, 7 to 10 minutes. Drain off the grease, leaving the ground beef and onion mixture in the pot.

2. Add diced tomatoes, tomato sauce, ketchup, water, kidney beans, chili seasoning mix, celery, Worcestershire sauce, and sugar and stir to combine.

3. Secure the lid and make sure the valve is pointing up to SEALING.

4. Press MANUAL (or press PRESSURE COOK and select HIGH PRESSURE) and adjust time to 10 minutes.

5. When multicooker signals the end of cooking time, press CANCEL, and then quick release the pressure by turning the valve down to VENTING with the handle of a wooden spoon or other device to prevent the steam from burning your hands during the release.

6. Remove the lid and stir. Serve while warm, topped with cheese and corn chips, if desired.

# SEVEN-CAN TORTILLA SOUP

Prep time: 5 minutes | Pressurization and cooking time: 15 minutes | Total time: 20 minutes | Yields: 6 to 8 servings

1 (15-ounce) can black beans, drained and rinsed

1 (15-ounce) can pinto beans, drained and rinsed

1 (14.5-ounce) can diced tomatoes, drained

1 (15-ounce) can sweet corn, drained

1 (12.5-ounce) can chicken breast, drained

1 (10-ounce) can green enchilada sauce

1 (14-ounce) can chicken broth

1 (1.25-ounce) packet taco seasoning

1 teaspoon ground cumin

1 teaspoon chili powder

1 teaspoon garlic powder

¼ teaspoon ground black pepper

Tortilla chips, for topping

Shredded cheddar cheese, for topping

Sour cream, for topping

Diced avocados

1. Add beans, tomatoes, corn, canned chicken, enchilada sauce, chicken broth, taco seasoning, cumin, chili powder, garlic powder, and pepper to the insert of a multicooker and stir to combine.

2. Secure the lid and make sure the valve is pointing up to SEALING.

3. Press MANUAL (or press PRESSURE COOK and select HIGH PRESSURE) and adjust time to 4 minutes.

4. When multicooker signals the end of cooking time, press CANCEL, and then quick release the pressure by turning the valve down to VENTING with the handle of a wooden spoon or other device to prevent the steam from burning your hands during the release.

5. Serve topped with tortilla chips, shredded cheese, sour cream, and diced avocados.

# MINESTRONE SOUP

Prep time: 15 minutes | Pressurization and cooking time: 31 minutes | Total time: 45 minutes | Yields: 8 to 10 servings

1 pound ground beef

1 onion, diced

1 medium zucchini, diced

2 stalks celery, sliced

3 russet potatoes, peeled and cubed

2 cups sliced carrots

1 teaspoon minced garlic

1 (14.5-ounce) can diced tomatoes, undrained

1 tablespoon Italian seasoning

3 cups tomato juice

1 (15-ounce) can dark red kidney beans, drained and rinsed

1 (15.5-ounce) can cannellini beans, drained and rinsed

1 (14.5-ounce) can cut green beans, drained

1 cup ditalini pasta

4 cups beef broth, divided

Salt and pepper, to taste

1. Press SAUTÉ to heat multicooker insert; add ground beef and use a wooden spoon to break up meat. Cook 2 minutes, then add chopped onion and sauté with ground beef until meat is cooked through and onions are tender, about 5 minutes. Drain off grease and return insert to multicooker.

2. Add zucchini, celery, potatoes, and carrots and stir well.

3. Add garlic and canned tomatoes in their juices, followed by Italian seasoning, tomato juice, kidney beans, cannellini beans, and green beans. Stir gently to combine.

4. Add pasta and 2 cups of the beef broth, then give the soup another gentle stir. Press CANCEL.

5. Secure the lid and make sure the valve is pointing up to SEALING.

6. Press MANUAL (or press PRESSURE COOK and select HIGH PRESSURE) and adjust time to 6 minutes.

7. When multicooker signals the end of cooking time, let pressure naturally release 10 minutes and then carefully turn the valve to VENTING to quick release remaining pressure.

8. Remove the lid and stir gently, adding up to 2 cups more beef broth until soup reaches desired consistency.

9. Season with salt and pepper to taste and serve.

# EASY LASAGNA SOUP

Prep time: 20 minutes | Pressurization and cooking time: 20 minutes | Total time: 40 minutes | Yields: 6 to 8 servings

1 pound Italian sausage

Pinch red pepper flakes

1 onion, chopped

2 teaspoons Italian seasoning

1 teaspoon dried basil

1 teaspoon dried oregano

1 teaspoon salt

½ teaspoon ground black pepper

5 cloves garlic, minced

4 ounces mushrooms, sliced

1 cup chopped carrots

1 (28-ounce) can crushed tomatoes

1 (14-ounce) can tomato sauce

4 to 5 cups chicken broth

9 lasagna noodles, broke in small pieces, about 1.5 inches long

1 cup shredded mozzarella cheese

1 (6-ounce) bag baby spinach, rinsed

1 cup cottage or ricotta cheese

Shredded Parmesan cheese, for topping.

1. Press SAUTÉ to heat multicooker insert; add sausage and red pepper flakes and use a wooden spoon to break up meat. Cook until browned, about 5 to 7 minutes.

2. Add the onion, Italian seasoning, basil, oregano, salt, and pepper. Cook until onion begins to turn translucent, stirring occasionally, about 3 minutes.

3. Add garlic and mushrooms and cook 1 minute, stirring frequently.

4. Mix in carrots, tomatoes, tomato sauce, and 4 to 5 cups broth, depending on how thick or thin you'd like the soup. Add broken up lasagna pieces and mix well. Press CANCEL.

5. Secure the lid and make sure the valve is pointing up to SEALING.

6. Press MANUAL (or press PRESSURE COOK and select HIGH PRESSURE) and adjust time to 6 minutes.

7. When multicooker signals the end of cooking time, press CANCEL, and then quick release the pressure by turning the valve down to VENTING with the handle of a wooden spoon or other device to prevent the steam from burning your hands during the release.

8. Remove lid and stir the soup to separate any noodles that are stuck together. Stir in mozzarella until cheese melts. Add spinach and cottage or ricotta cheese and stir again.

9. Serve in bowls topped with shredded Parmesan cheese.

# TOMATO-BACON BISQUE

Prep time: 15 minutes | Pressurization and cooking time: 30 to 35 minutes | Total time: 45 to 50 minutes | Yields: 4 to 6 servings

| | | | | |
|---|---|---|---|---|
| 1 | tablespoon butter | | 1 | tablespoon Old Bay Seasoning |
| ½ | cup finely diced carrots | | ½ | teaspoon dried oregano |
| ½ | cup finely diced celery | | ½ | teaspoon dried parsley |
| 6 | green onions, finely diced | | 1 | teaspoon ground black pepper |
| 2 | cloves garlic, minced | | ½ | teaspoon paprika |
| 1 | (28-ounce) can petite diced tomatoes | | 1 | cup heavy cream |
| 4 | cups low-sodium chicken broth | | 6 | slices bacon, cooked and crumbled |

1. Place butter in the insert of a multicooker and press SAUTÉ.

2. When butter has melted, add carrots, celery, onions, and garlic to the insert and sauté 7 to 8 minutes, until vegetables have softened slightly. Press CANCEL.

3. Add diced tomatoes, chicken broth, Old Bay, oregano, parsley, pepper, and paprika. Stir briefly.

4. Secure the lid and make sure the valve is pointing up to SEALING.

5. Press MANUAL (or press PRESSURE COOK and select HIGH PRESSURE) and adjust time to 8 minutes.

6. When multicooker signals the end of cooking time, let pressure naturally release until all steam has dispersed, about 10 to 15 minutes.

7. Remove lid and then use an immersion blender to puree the mixture. Alternatively, transfer soup to the bowl of a food processor and puree until smooth.

8. Stir in cream and bacon pieces and serve immediately, garnished with green onions.

# BROCCOLI CHEDDAR SOUP

Prep time: 15 minutes | Pressurization and cooking time: 20 minutes | Total time: 35 minutes | Yields: 6 to 8 servings

| | | | |
|---|---|---|---|
| 1 | tablespoon olive oil | ¼ | teaspoon ground nutmeg |
| 1 | onion, diced | 1½ | cups heavy cream |
| 3 | cups chicken broth | 2 | cups shredded cheddar cheese |
| 4 | cups chopped broccoli | 1 | tablespoon hot sauce |
| ½ | cup shredded carrots | | |

1. Add olive oil to the insert of a multicooker and press SAUTÉ.

2. When oil is hot and rippling, add onions and sauté until they become soft and translucent, about 5 minutes.

3. Press CANCEL then add chicken broth, broccoli, carrots, and nutmeg. Stir gently.

4. Secure the lid and make sure the valve is pointing up to SEALING.

5. Press MANUAL (or press PRESSURE COOK and select HIGH PRESSURE) and adjust time to 4 minutes.

6. When multicooker signals the end of cooking time, press CANCEL, and then quick release the pressure by turning the valve down to VENTING with the handle of a wooden spoon or other device to prevent the steam from burning your hands during the release.

7. Remove the lid and stir in the cream.

8. Press SAUTÉ and stir in the shredded cheese and hot sauce until cheese melts and everything is combined well, being careful not to let the soup boil.

9. Serve immediately.

# POTATO SOUP

Prep time: 10 minutes | Pressurization and cooking time: 33 to 38 minutes | Total time: 43 to 48 minutes | Yields: 8 to 10 servings

---

3   pounds russet potatoes, peeled and diced into ½-inch cubes

1   medium yellow onion, diced

6   cups low-sodium chicken broth

½   teaspoon garlic powder

½   teaspoon seasoned salt

½   teaspoon ground black pepper

Pinch dried parsley

⅓   cup all-purpose flour

2   cups heavy cream, divided

1   cup shredded Parmesan cheese, divided

12   strips bacon, cooked and crumbled

2   tablespoons fresh minced parsley

1. Place potatoes, onion, chicken broth, garlic powder, seasoned salt, pepper, and dried parsley into the insert of a multicooker.

2. Secure the lid and make sure the valve is pointing up to SEALING.

3. Press MANUAL (or press PRESSURE COOK and select HIGH PRESSURE) and adjust time to 15 minutes.

4. When multicooker signals the end of cooking time, press CANCEL, and then quick release the pressure by turning the valve down to VENTING with the handle of a wooden spoon or other device to prevent the steam from burning your hands during the release.

5. In a small bowl, whisk together flour and 1/2 cup of the cream until smooth.

6. Remove lid from multicooker, press SAUTÉ, then stir in cream and flour mixture.

7. Stir in 3/4 cup of the cheese, the bacon, and remaining cream. Cook, stirring constantly, 6 to 8 minutes until the soup thickens.

8. Ladle soup into bowls and top each individual serving with a sprinkle of remaining Parmesan cheese and some chopped fresh parsley.

# side dishes

# HONEY-GLAZED CARROTS

Prep time: 5 minutes | Pressurization and cooking time: 18 minutes | Total time: 23 minutes | Yields: 6 servings

2 pounds carrots, peeled and cut in ¼-inch slices

1 cup water

3 tablespoons olive oil

3 tablespoons honey

Salt and pepper, to taste

Chopped fresh parsley, for garnishing

1. Add carrots and water to the insert of a multicooker.

2. Secure the lid and make sure the valve is pointing up to SEALING.

3. Press MANUAL (or press PRESSURE COOK and select HIGH PRESSURE) and adjust time to 3 minutes.

4. When multicooker signals the end of cooking time, quick release the pressure by turning the valve down to VENTING with the handle of a wooden spoon or other device to prevent the steam from burning your hands during the release.

5. Remove lid and drain excess water from insert.

6. Add olive oil, honey, and salt and pepper to taste to the insert, tossing well to coat carrots. Press CANCEL to turn off multicooker.

7. Serve, garnished with fresh chopped parsley.

# LEMON-PARMESAN BROCCOLI

Prep time: 5 minutes | Pressurization and cooking time: 10 to 15 minutes | Total time: 15 to 20 minutes | Yields: 6 servings

| | |
|---|---|
| **4** | **cups broccoli florets** |
| **½** | **cup water** |
| **1** | **tablespoon butter** |

| | |
|---|---|
| **2** | **tablespoons lemon juice** |
| **2** | **tablespoons shredded Parmesan cheese** |
| | **Salt and pepper, to taste** |

1. Put broccoli and water in the insert of a multicooker.

2. Secure the lid and make sure the valve is pointing up to SEALING.

3. Press MANUAL (or press PRESSURE COOK and select HIGH PRESSURE) and adjust time to 0 minutes (The broccoli will cook while the multicooker pressurizes.)

4. When multicooker signals the end of cooking time, quick release the pressure by turning the valve down to VENTING with the handle of a wooden spoon or other device to prevent the steam from burning your hands during the release.

5. Remove lid and quickly transfer broccoli to a colander; run broccoli briefly under cold water to stop the cooking process.

6. Drain water from the multicooker insert and return broccoli to the insert.

7. Add lemon juice and Parmesan cheese and toss to coat the broccoli.

8. Season with salt and pepper, to taste. Press CANCEL to turn off multicooker.

9. Serve immediately.

# PARMESAN BROCCOLI ORZO

Prep time: 10 minutes | Pressurization and cooking time: 20 minutes | Total time: 30 minutes | Yields: 4 to 6 servings

---

2 cups chicken broth

8 ounces (1½ cups) orzo pasta

1 to 2 cups roughly chopped broccoli

2 tablespoons butter

4 cloves garlic, minced

1 teaspoon salt

½ teaspoon ground black pepper

1½ cups shredded Parmesan cheese, plus more for topping

1. Place chicken broth, orzo pasta, and broccoli in the insert of a multicooker and stir to combine.

2. Secure the lid and make sure the valve is pointing up to SEALING.

3. Press MANUAL (or press PRESSURE COOK and select HIGH PRESSURE) and adjust time to 5 minutes.

4. When multicooker signals the end of cooking time, press CANCEL, and then quick release the pressure by turning the valve down to VENTING with the handle of a wooden spoon or other device to prevent the steam from burning your hands during the release.

5. Remove lid and add butter, garlic, salt, pepper, and shredded Parmesan cheese; stir until butter and cheese have melted and everything is thoroughly combined.

6. Serve, topped with additional shredded Parmesan cheese.

# BACON BRUSSELS SPROUTS

Prep time: 10 minutes | Pressurization and cooking time: 15 to 20 minutes | Total time: 25 to 30 minutes | Yields: 4 servings

1   cup water

1   pound Brussels sprouts, halved

1   tablespoon olive oil

½   onion, diced

½   pound bacon, diced

1   teaspoon salt

½   teaspoon ground black pepper

1. Pour 1 cup water in the insert of a multicooker and then place steamer basket in the bottom of the insert. Add Brussels sprouts to the steamer basket.

2. Secure the lid and make sure the valve is pointing up to SEALING.

3. Press MANUAL (or press PRESSURE COOK and select HIGH PRESSURE) and adjust time to 2 minutes.

4. When multicooker signals the end of cooking time, press CANCEL, and then quick release the pressure by turning the valve down to VENTING with the handle of a wooden spoon or other device to prevent the steam from burning your hands during the release.

5. Remove lid, transfer Brussels sprouts to a large bowl, and drain liquid from the insert.

6. Return insert to the multicooker, add olive oil to the insert, and press SAUTÉ.

7. When oil is hot and rippling, add onions and bacon and sauté until onion is translucent and bacon starts to crisp, about 8 minutes. Add Brussels sprouts back to the multicooker, season with salt and pepper, and sauté 1 to 2 minutes to meld flavors and heat everything through.

# BUFFALO CAULIFLOWER

Prep time: 5 minutes | Pressurization and cooking time: 20 minutes | Total time: 25 minutes | Yields: 4 servings

| | | | |
|---|---|---|---|
| 1 | head cauliflower | 1½ | teaspoons garlic salt |
| ¾ | cup buffalo sauce, such as Frank's RedHot Wings Buffalo Sauce | 1 | cup water |
| ¼ | cup butter, melted | | Ranch or bleu cheese dressing, for passing |

1. Trim all leaves from cauliflower head and wash thoroughly; set cauliflower head on cutting board until ready to baste with buffalo sauce.

2. In a small bowl, whisk together the buffalo sauce, melted butter, and garlic salt until well combined.

3. Brush half of the sauce over the cauliflower.

4. Place trivet in the insert of a multicooker and pour in 1 cup water.

5. Place basted cauliflower on trivet, secure the lid, and make sure the valve is pointing up to SEALING.

6. Press MANUAL (or press PRESSURE COOK and select HIGH PRESSURE) and adjust time to 2 minutes.

7. When multicooker signals the end of cooking time, press CANCEL, and then quick release the pressure by turning the valve down to VENTING with the handle of a wooden spoon or other device to prevent the steam from burning your hands during the release.

8. Heat oven broiler to high.

9. Remove the multicooker lid and carefully transfer cauliflower to cutting board; cut cauliflower into bite-sized pieces and arrange in an even layer on a large baking sheet.

10. Brush remaining buffalo sauce over the cauliflower pieces and broil 2 minutes.

11. Serve hot with ranch or bleu cheese dressing for dipping.

# CHEESY CAULIFLOWER

Prep time: 10 minutes | Pressurization and cooking time: 17 to 20 minutes | Total time: 27 to 30 minutes | Yields: 4 servings

½ cup cold water

1 head cauliflower, chopped into florets

2 tablespoons butter

2 tablespoons all-purpose flour

½ teaspoon salt

1⅓ cups milk

1 cup shredded sharp cheddar cheese

1. Pour ½ cup cold water in the insert of a multicooker and place a steamer basket inside the insert. Put cauliflower florets into the steamer basket.

2. Secure the lid and make sure the valve is pointing up to SEALING.

3. Press MANUAL (or press PRESSURE COOK and select HIGH PRESSURE) and adjust time to 2 minutes.

4. When multicooker signals the end of cooking time, press CANCEL, and then quick release the pressure by turning the valve down to VENTING with the handle of a wooden spoon or other device to prevent the steam from burning your hands during the release.

5. Remove lid and carefully transfer steamer basket with cauliflower to the countertop. Drain water from insert and return insert to multicooker.

6. Add butter to the insert and press SAUTÉ.

7. When butter has melted, whisk in flour and salt and stir constantly 1 minute.

8. Whisk in milk and cook until sauce is thickened, about 2 to 3 minutes. Stir in cheese all at once, and continue stirring until melted, about 30 to 60 seconds.

9. Add cooked cauliflower back to the insert and stir until all the cauliflower is covered with cheese sauce. Serve warm.

# GREEN BEAN & BACON CASSEROLE

Prep time: 5 minutes | Pressurization and cooking time: 25 to 30 minutes | Total time: 30 to 35 minutes | Yields: 4

½   cup milk

2   (10.5-ounce) cans cream of mushroom soup

2   (14.5-ounce) cans green beans

1¼   cups French's Original Fried Onions

10   slices bacon, cooked and crumbled

1. Spray the insert of a multicooker with nonstick cooking spray.

2. In a medium bowl, whisk together milk and cream of mushroom soup. Fold in green beans until well combined and pour into multicooker insert.

3. Secure the lid and make sure the valve is pointing up to SEALING.

4. Press MANUAL (or press PRESSURE COOK and select HIGH PRESSURE) and adjust time to 1 minute.

5. When multicooker signals the end of cooking time, press CANCEL, and then quick release the pressure by turning the valve down to VENTING with the handle of a wooden spoon or other device to prevent the steam from burning your hands during the release.

6. Remove lid and stir in half of the fried onions.

7. Sprinkle bacon and remaining fried onions on top, then serve and enjoy.

# CREAMED CORN

Prep time: 5 minutes | Pressurization and cooking time: 25 to 30 minutes | Total time: 30 to 35 minutes | Yields: 10 servings

2  (16-ounce) bags frozen corn

1  (8-ounce) brick cream cheese

½  cup (1 stick) butter

½  cup milk

½  cup heavy cream

1  tablespoon granulated sugar

Salt and pepper, to taste

1. Add all ingredients to the insert of a multicooker.

2. Secure the lid and make sure the valve is pointing up to SEALING.

3. Press MANUAL (or press PRESSURE COOK and select HIGH PRESSURE) and adjust time to 15 minutes.

4. When multicooker signals the end of cooking time, press CANCEL, and then quick release the pressure by turning the valve down to VENTING with the handle of a wooden spoon or other device to prevent the steam from burning your hands during the release.

5. Remove lid, stir, and serve warm.

# GARLIC MUSHROOMS

Prep time: 10 minutes | Pressurization and cooking time: 20 minutes | Total time: 30 minutes | Yields: 8 to 10 servings

2   **pounds fresh small mushrooms**

1   **onion, diced**

4   **cloves garlic, minced**

1   **cup beef broth**

3   **tablespoons balsamic vinegar**

3   **tablespoons olive oil**

1   **teaspoon salt**

1   **teaspoon dried basil**

½   **teaspoon fresh ground black pepper**

    **Dash red pepper flakes**

1. Place mushrooms, onions, and garlic in the insert of a multicooker.

2. In a large mixing bowl, stir together broth, vinegar, olive oil, salt, basil, pepper, and red pepper flakes. Pour mixture on top of mushrooms in the multicooker insert.

3. Secure the lid and make sure the valve is pointing up to SEALING.

4. Press MANUAL (or press PRESSURE COOK and select HIGH PRESSURE) and adjust time to 5 minutes.

5. When multicooker signals the end of cooking time, press CANCEL, and then quick release the pressure by turning the valve down to VENTING with the handle of a wooden spoon or other device to prevent the steam from burning your hands during the release.

6. Remove lid from multicooker, transfer mushrooms to a serving bowl, and serve while still warm.

# BACON-RANCH POTATOES

Prep time: 10 minutes | Pressurization and cooking time: 25 to 30 minutes | Total time: 3 minutes | Yields: 6 servings

3 strips bacon, chopped

2 pounds yellow potatoes, peeled and cut into 1-inch cubes

2 teaspoons dried parsley flakes

1 teaspoon salt

1 teaspoon garlic powder

⅓ cup water

1 cup shredded cheddar cheese

⅓ cup ranch dressing

1. Press SAUTÉ to heat multicooker insert; add bacon to the pot and cook and stir until bacon is crispy, about 8 minutes. Press CANCEL.

2. Add potatoes, parsley flakes, salt, and garlic powder to insert then pour in ⅓ cup water.

3. Secure the lid and make sure the valve is pointing up to SEALING.

4. Press MANUAL (or press PRESSURE COOK and select HIGH PRESSURE) and adjust time to 7 minutes.

5. When multicooker signals the end of cooking time, press CANCEL, and then quick release the pressure by turning the valve down to VENTING with the handle of a wooden spoon or other device to prevent the steam from burning your hands during the release.

6. Remove lid, stir in cheese and ranch dressing to combine, and serve warm.

# GARLIC MASHED POTATOES

Prep time: 10 minutes | Pressurization and cooking time: 25 minutes | Total time: 35 minutes | Yields: 6 servings

---

- **8** red potatoes, peeled and cut into ¼-inch slices
- **5** cups water
- **1** teaspoon salt
- **¼** cup butter, cut into pieces

- **¼** cup sour cream
- **¼** cup half and half, warmed
- **½** teaspoon garlic powder
- Salt and pepper, to taste
- Minced chives, for garnishing

1. Place potato slices in the insert of a multicooker.

2. Pour water over potatoes and sprinkle on 1 teaspoon salt.

3. Secure the lid and make sure the valve is pointing up to SEALING.

4. Press MANUAL (or press PRESSURE COOK and select HIGH PRESSURE) and adjust time to 8 minutes.

5. When multicooker signals the end of cooking time, press CANCEL, and then quick release the pressure by turning the valve down to VENTING with the handle of a wooden spoon or other device to prevent the steam from burning your hands during the release.

6. Remove lid and drain off water.

7. Add butter, sour cream, half and half, garlic powder, and salt and pepper to taste. Mash with a potato masher or fork until smooth.

8. Serve immediately, garnished with minced chives if desired.

# POTATO SALAD

Prep time: 15 minutes | Pressurization and cooking time: 20 minutes | Total time: 45 minutes | Yields: 6 servings

4   cups russet potatoes, peeled and cubed

4   cups water

1   teaspoon salt, plus more for adjusting flavors

4   eggs

1   cup mayonnaise

1   tablespoon yellow mustard

½   tablespoon garlic powder

1   tablespoon apple cider vinegar

1   teaspoon granulated sugar

½   teaspoon onion powder

Ground black pepper, to taste

½   teaspoon dill weed

3   stalks celery, diced

¾   cup chopped sweet pickles

½   cup chopped red onion

½   teaspoon McCormick Perfect Pinch Salad Supreme Seasoning

1. Add cubed potatoes, water, and 1 teaspoon salt to the insert of a multicooker and stir gently.

2. Carefully place the 4 eggs on top of the potatoes. (They will hard cook at the same time as the potatoes.)

3. Secure the lid and make sure the valve is pointing up to SEALING.

4. Press MANUAL (or press PRESSURE COOK and select HIGH PRESSURE) and adjust time to 3 minutes.

5. When multicooker signals the end of cooking time, let pressure naturally release 2 minutes and then carefully turn the valve to VENTING to quick release remaining pressure.

6. Fill a medium bowl with ice and water. Remove multicooker lid and carefully transfer eggs to the bowl of ice water; set aside.

7. Drain excess liquid from the insert and transfer potatoes to a baking sheet to cool; set aside.

8. Prepare potato salad dressing: In a large mixing bowl combine the mayonnaise, mustard, garlic powder, apple cider vinegar, sugar, onion powder, pepper, and dill weed. Stir until well blended. Taste and add salt or other seasonings as needed.

9. When eggs are cool to the touch, peel and dice 3 of them. Add the eggs to the mayo mixture and stir in gently.

10. Add in the cooled potatoes, celery, pickles, and onions and fold in gently until combined well.

11. Peel and slice the 4th egg and lay the slices on top of the salad.

12. Sprinkle the Salad Supreme over the top of the salad, cover, and refrigerate until ready to serve.

# GARLIC PARMESAN SPAGHETTI SQUASH

Prep time: 5 minutes | Pressurization and cooking time: 25 minutes | Total time: 30 minutes | Yields: 4 servings

1 cup water

1 (3-pound) spaghetti squash

1 tablespoon olive oil

3 cloves garlic, minced

½ cup finely grated parmesan cheese

Chopped fresh parsley, for garnishing

1. Pour 1 cup water in the insert of a multicooker and then place steamer basket in the bottom of the insert.

2. Slice the spaghetti squash in half, scoop the seeds out from the center, and discard seeds. Place the spaghetti squash on top of the steamer rack.

3. Secure the lid and make sure the valve is pointing up to SEALING.

4. Press MANUAL (or press PRESSURE COOK and select HIGH PRESSURE) and adjust time to 7 minutes.

5. When multicooker signals the end of cooking time, press CANCEL, and then quick release the pressure by turning the valve down to VENTING with the handle of a wooden spoon or other device to prevent the steam from burning your hands during the release.

6. Remove the lid and transfer squash to a cutting board. Use the tines of a fork to separate the cooked strands from the hard shell; discard shells.

7. Drain excess water from the insert and return insert to pot.

8. Add olive oil to the insert and press SAUTÉ.

9. When oil is hot and rippling, add garlic and sauté until fragrant, about 30 seconds. Add strands of spaghetti squash back to the pot, along with Parmesan cheese. Stir until heated through and cheese is melted.

10. Serve immediately, garnished with fresh, chopped parsley.

# LOADED BAKED SWEET POTATOES

Prep time: 5 minutes | Pressurization and cooking time: 25 to 40 minutes, depending on size of potatoes | Total time: 30 to 45 minutes | Yields: 4 servings

1   cup water

4   sweet potatoes, washed and scrubbed
    Salt and pepper, to taste

2   tablespoons butter

½   cup plus 2 tablespoons sour cream

5   tablespoons bacon bits

½   cup plus 2 tablespoons shredded
    cheddar cheese

1½  tablespoon dried chives

1. Pour 1 cup water into the insert of a multicooker and place trivet in the bottom of the insert.

2. Pierce each potato 5 to 6 times with a fork. This allows for steam to escape from the potatoes while they cook.

3. Arrange sweet potatoes on top of the trivet and season with salt and pepper.

4. Secure the lid and make sure the valve is pointing up to SEALING.

5. Press MANUAL (or press PRESSURE COOK and select HIGH PRESSURE) and adjust time to 15 minutes for small potatoes (about 2 inches in diameter), 22 for medium potatoes (about 3 inches in diameter), or 30 for large potatoes (about 4 inches in diameter).

6. When multicooker signals the end of cooking time, let pressure naturally release for 10 minutes and then carefully turn the valve to VENTING to quick release remaining pressure.

7. Remove lid and transfer potatoes from multicooker to a serving platter.

8. Slice potatoes in half and top with butter, sour cream, bacon bits, cheddar cheese, and dried chives.

# PERFECTLY STEAMED VEGETABLES

Prep time: 5 minutes | Pressurization and cooking time: 16 minutes | Total time: 21 minutes | Yields: 8 servings

4   carrots, peeled and cut into 1-inch lengths

1   red bell pepper, chopped

1   yellow bell pepper, chopped

1   head cauliflower, chopped

1   head broccoli, chopped

1   cup water

Garlic salt, to taste

Rosemary, to taste

1. Place carrots, bell peppers, cauliflower, and broccoli in the insert of a multicooker. Pour water over vegetables.

2. Secure the lid and make sure the valve is pointing up to SEALING.

3. Press MANUAL (or press PRESSURE COOK and select HIGH PRESSURE) and adjust time to 1 minute.

4. When multicooker signals the end of cooking time, press CANCEL, and then quick release the pressure by turning the valve down to VENTING with the handle of a wooden spoon or other device to prevent the steam from burning your hands during the release.

5. Remove lid and transfer vegetables to a serving bowl using a slotted spoon.

6. Sprinkle with garlic salt and dried rosemary to taste, and serve warm.

# BBQ BAKED BEANS

Prep time: 15 minutes | Pressurization and cooking time: 1 hour 40 minutes | Total time: 1 hour 55 minutes | Yields: 10 servings

| | |
|---|---|
| 2 cups great northern beans | ½ cup ketchup |
| 8 cups water | ½ cup BBQ sauce |
| 1 teaspoon salt | 1 (4-ounce) can diced green chiles |
| 8 slices thick-cut bacon, chopped | ¼ cup pure maple syrup |
| ½ medium onion, diced (optional) | 2 teaspoons Dijon mustard |

1. Add beans, water, and salt to the insert of a multicooker.

2. Secure the lid and make sure the valve is pointing up to SEALING.

3. Press MANUAL (or press PRESSURE COOK and select HIGH PRESSURE) and adjust time to 25 minutes.

4. When multicooker signals the end of cooking time, let pressure naturally release.

5. Remove the lid and pour the beans into a mesh strainer; rinse with cold water and set aside.

6. Press SAUTÉ to heat the multicooker insert. Once hot, add bacon and cook stirring occasionally, until bacon starts to brown, about 5 minutes.

7. Drain off all but 1 tablespoon of the bacon grease, add the onions, and sauté until onions are tender and bacon is crisped, about 5 more minutes. Press CANCEL.

8. Add ketchup, BBQ sauce, chiles, syrup, and mustard to the pot and stir well, making sure to scrape the bottom of the insert and bring up any browned or stuck-on bits. Return beans to the insert and stir until completely combined.

9. Secure the lid and make sure the valve is pointing up to SEALING.

10. Press MANUAL (or press PRESSURE COOK and select HIGH PRESSURE) and adjust time to 15 minutes.

11. When multicooker signals the end of cooking time, let pressure naturally release.

12. Remove lid, stir, and serve warm.

# REFRIED BEANS

Prep time: 10 minutes | Pressurization and cooking time: 1 hour 25 minutes | Total time: 1 hour 30 minutes | Yields: 10 servings

2  cups dry pinto beans

1  medium onion, diced

3  cloves garlic, minced

1  teaspoon salt

1  (4-ounce) can green chilies

4  cups chicken stock

3  cups water

1  teaspoon cumin

½  teaspoon chili powder

½  teaspoon ground black pepper

1. Place pinto beans in a colander and rinse, removing any debris.  Drain off water and place beans in the insert of a multicooker.

2. Add the onion, garlic, salt, green chilies, chicken stock, water, cumin, chili powder, and pepper.

3. Secure the lid and make sure the valve is pointing up to SEALING.

4. Press MANUAL (or press PRESSURE COOK and select HIGH PRESSURE) and adjust time to 45 minutes.

5. When multicooker signals the end of cooking time, let pressure naturally release 20 minutes and then carefully turn the valve to VENTING to quick release remaining pressure.

6. Drain the beans, reserving some of the liquid. Return the beans to the empty pot and mash with a potato masher or puree with an immersion blender, depending on how smooth you like your beans. Add reserved liquid as needed to reach desired texture. Taste and adjust seasonings as needed.

# CILANTRO-LIME RICE

Prep time: 5 minutes | Pressurization and cooking time: 25 minutes | Total time: 30 minutes | Yields: 6 servings

| | |
|---|---|
| 1 | cup long grain white rice |
| 1¼ | cups water |
| 2 | tablespoons vegetable oil |
| ½ | teaspoon salt |

| | |
|---|---|
| | Zest of 1 lime |
| 1 | tablespoon freshly squeezed lime juice |
| 3 | tablespoons freshly chopped cilantro |

1. Add rice, water, vegetable oil, and salt to the insert of a multicooker.

2. Secure the lid and make sure the valve is pointing up to SEALING.

3. Press MANUAL (or press PRESSURE COOK and select HIGH PRESSURE) and adjust time to 7 minutes.

4. When multicooker signals the end of cooking time, press CANCEL, and then quick release the pressure by turning the valve down to VENTING with the handle of a wooden spoon or other device to prevent the steam from burning your hands during the release.

5. Remove lid and transfer rice to a large bowl.

6. Fluff rice with a fork then stir in lime zest, lime juice, and cilantro. Serve immediately.

# FRENCH ONION RICE

Prep time: 10 minutes | Pressurization and cooking time: 15 to 20 minutes | Total time: 25 to 30 minutes | Yields: 4 servings

2　cups long grain white rice, rinsed until water runs clear

2½　cups water

1　(1-ounce) packet French onion soup mix

1. Place rice, water, and French onion soup mix in the insert of a multicooker and stir well to combine.

2. Secure the lid and make sure the valve is pointing up to SEALING.

3. Press MANUAL (or press PRESSURE COOK and select HIGH PRESSURE) and adjust time to 7 minutes.

4. When multicooker signals the end of cooking time, press CANCEL, and then quick release the pressure by turning the valve down to VENTING with the handle of a wooden spoon or other device to prevent the steam from burning your hands during the release.

5. Remove lid, fluff rice with a fork, and serve.

# LEMON RICE PILAF

Prep time: 10 minutes | Pressurization and cooking time: 40 minutes | Total time: 50 minutes | Yields: 6 servings

| | |
|---|---|
| 2 | tablespoons butter |
| 1 | teaspoon minced garlic |
| ½ | cup chopped onion |
| 2 | cups long grain white rice |

| | |
|---|---|
| 1¾ | cups chicken broth |
| ¼ | cup lemon juice |
| 1 | teaspoon salt |
| | Fresh chopped parsley, for garnishing |

1. Place butter in the insert of a multicooker and press SAUTÉ.

2. When butter has melted, add garlic and onion and sauté until garlic is fragrant and onions have started to become translucent, about 5 minutes.

3. Add rice and continue stirring until rice is coated in butter and begins to turn clear, about 2–3 minutes.

4. Add chicken broth, lemon juice, and salt, and stir until mixed.

5. Secure the lid and make sure the valve is pointing up to SEALING.

6. Press MANUAL and adjust time to 7 minutes.

7. When multicooker signals the end of cooking time, press CANCEL, and then quick release the pressure by turning the valve down to VENTING with the handle of a wooden spoon or other device to prevent the steam from burning your hands during the release.

8. Remove lid, stir, and serve, garnished with fresh parsley.

# GRANDMA'S STUFFING

Prep time: 15 minutes | Pressurization and cooking time: 45 minutes | Total time: 1 hour | Yields: 6 to 8 servings

½ cup (1 stick) butter

1 cup diced celery

1 cup diced onion

1 cup diced sweet apples, such as Honeycrisp

¾ cup fresh sliced mushrooms

½ teaspoon ground sage

⅛ teaspoon dried thyme

⅛ teaspoon fresh ground black pepper

1 cup chicken broth

10 ounces cubed, seasoned stuffing

1 cup water

1. Add butter to the insert of a multicooker and press SAUTÉ.

2. When butter has melted, stir in celery, onion, apples, mushrooms, sage, thyme, and pepper and sauté 2 minutes, until vegetables begin to soften. Press CANCEL.

3. In a large bowl, add stuffing, chicken broth, and softened vegetables and apples from the multicooker. Mix until stuffing has soaked in the broth and is well combined with herbs and vegetables.

4. Wipe out multicooker insert with a damp cloth so no food remnants burn while stuffing cooks.

5. Spray a deep, 7-inch cake pan, such as the Instant Pot Official Round Cake Pan, with nonstick cooking spray. Carefully spread stuffing mixture in pan, being sure to not pack it tightly.

6. Pour 1 cup water in the insert and place the trivet in the insert. Place pan with stuffing on the trivet.

7. Secure the lid and make sure the valve is pointing up to SEALING.

8. Press MANUAL (or press PRESSURE COOK and select HIGH PRESSURE) and adjust time to 10 minutes.

9. When multicooker signals the end of cooking time, let pressure naturally release.

10. Serve as is or, if you want a more golden top, place pan in a 400-degree F. oven for a few minutes to brown the stuffing.

# CORNBREAD

Prep time: 10 minutes | Pressurization and cooking time: 50 minutes | Total time: 1 hour | Yields: 6 servings

⅔ cup all-purpose flour

½ cup cornmeal

½ cup granulated sugar

1 tablespoon baking powder

½ teaspoon salt

1 large egg

⅓ cup half and half

3 tablespoons butter, melted

1½ cups water

1. In a large mixing bowl, whisk together flour, cornmeal, sugar, baking powder, and salt. Stir in egg, half and half, and butter until just combined. Do not overmix.

2. Spray a 7-inch springform pan with nonstick cooking spray, spread batter evenly in pan, and cover tightly with aluminum foil; set aside.

3. Place trivet in the insert of a multicooker and pour water over the trivet.

4. Carefully place covered pan of batter on top of the trivet, secure the multicooker lid, and make sure the valve is pointing up to SEALING.

5. Press MANUAL (or press PRESSURE COOK and select HIGH PRESSURE) and adjust time to 25 minutes.

6. When multicooker signals the end of cooking time, let pressure naturally release 10 minutes and then carefully turn the valve to VENTING to quick release remaining pressure.

7. Remove lid and carefully transfer pan to a cooling rack.

8. Remove foil, let cornbread cool briefly, then cut into slices and serve.

# MULTICOOKER DINNER ROLLS

Prep time: 55 minutes | Cooking time: 10 to 12 minutes | Total time: 1 hour 5 to 1 hour 7 minutes | Yields: 18 to 24 rolls

| | | | |
|---|---|---|---|
| 2 | cups milk | 1 | teaspoon salt |
| ½ | cup (1 stick) cold butter | 3 | eggs |
| 2 | tablespoons dry, active yeast | 7 | cups all-purpose flour |
| ½ | cup warm water | 1 | tablespoon oil |
| ¼ | cup plus ½ teaspoon granulated sugar | | |

1. Heat milk in a small saucepan over medium heat just until it starts to boil; remove from heat.

2. Place cold butter in hot milk and allow butter to melt; cool mixture to room temperature.

3. While milk cools, mix together warm water, yeast, and ½ teaspoon of the sugar in a small bowl. Let yeast rest 10 minutes, until frothy.

4. Pour room temperature milk and the yeast mixture into the bowl of an electric stand mixer fitted with the dough hook attachment.

5. Add remaining sugar, salt, and eggs and mix at low speed until combined.

6. Add 3 cups of the flour and mix until just combined, then add the remaining 4 cups flour and mix on low speed until all flour is incorporated. The dough will be very sticky.

7. Pour the 1 tablespoon oil into the insert of a multicooker and transfer dough to the pot. Turn dough to cover all sides with oil.

8. Press YOGURT and make sure output reads NORMAL.

9. Cover with a glass lid or plate and let dough proof 20 minutes. Don't use the regular multicooker lid that locks into place because the dough might rise too high and make a mess on the lid. A glass lid or plate will be much easier to clean if dough sticks to it.

10. Remove lid or plate and knead the dough for 1 minute while still inside the insert. Replace the lid and proof 10 more minutes. Press CANCEL to turn off multicooker.

11. Preheat oven to 450 degrees F. Spray a baking sheet with nonstick cooking spray or line with parchment paper.

12. Pinch off a small amount of dough and form it into a ball about the size of a golf ball. Place on prepared baking sheet and repeat until all dough has been used.

13. Let rolls rise 10 minutes before baking on the middle rack 10 minutes, until golden brown.

# CHEESY CRAB DIP

Prep time: 5 minutes | Pressurization and cooking time: 15 to 20 minutes | Total time: 20 to 25 minutes | Yields: 4 servings

| | |
|---|---|
| 1 **(8-ounce) brick cream cheese, softened** | 1 **teaspoon Worcestershire sauce** |
| ½ **cup mayonnaise** | 1 **cup shredded Colby Jack cheese** |
| ¼ **cup sour cream** | 1 **pound imitation crab meat** |
| 1 **teaspoon Old Bay Seasoning** | ½ **cup shredded cheddar cheese** |
| 2 **tablespoons lime juice** | ½ **cup shredded mozzarella cheese** |
| 1 **tablespoon Dijon mustard** | 1 **cup water** |

1. In a large bowl, mix together cream cheese, mayonnaise, sour cream, Old Bay Seasoning, lime juice, Dijon mustard, Worcestershire sauce, Colby Jack cheese, and crab meat.

2. Spray a 7-inch cake pan, such as the Instant Pot Official Round Cake Pan, with nonstick cooking spray, and pour the crab mixture into the pan, spreading it out evenly.

3. Sprinkle cheddar and mozzarella cheese on top, then cover pan tightly with aluminum foil.

4. Pour 1 cup water into the insert of a multicooker and place trivet in the insert. Place the covered pan of crab dip on top of the trivet.

5. Secure the lid and make sure the valve is pointing up to SEALING.

6. Press MANUAL (or press PRESSURE COOK and select HIGH PRESSURE) and adjust time to 5 minutes.

7. When multicooker signals the end of cooking time, press CANCEL, and then quick release the pressure by turning the valve down to VENTING with the handle of a wooden spoon or other device to prevent the steam from burning your hands during the release.

8. Heat oven broiler to high.

9. Remove the multicooker lid and transfer the pan of crab dip to the countertop. Remove foil from crab dip and broil 2 minutes, until top is browned and bubbly.

10. Serve warm with crackers, baguette slices, or pita chips.

# desserts and snacks

# CINNAMON APPLESAUCE

Prep time: 15 minutes | Pressurization and cooking time: 30 minutes | Total time: 45 minutes | Yields: 8 servings

---

3 pounds Granny Smith or golden delicious apples, peeled, cored, and cut into small chunks

¾ cup water

1 teaspoon ground cinnamon

1½ tablespoons brown sugar

Dash salt

1. Add apples, water, cinnamon, brown sugar, and salt to the insert of a multicooker and stir to roughly coat apples in cinnamon and brown sugar.

2. Secure the lid and make sure the valve is pointing up to SEALING.

3. Press MANUAL (or press PRESSURE COOK and select HIGH PRESSURE) and adjust time to 5 minutes.

4. When multicooker signals the end of cooking time, let pressure naturally release 10 minutes and then carefully turn the valve to VENTING to quick release remaining pressure.

5. Remove the lid, stir, and serve warm. Leftover applesauce can be stored in an air-tight container in the refrigerator 5 to 7 days.

# APPLE CRISP

Prep time: 20 minutes | Pressurization and cooking time: 16 minutes | Total time: 46 minutes | Yields: 6 servings

| | | | |
|---|---|---|---|
| 6 | Granny Smith apples, peeled and diced | ⅛ | teaspoon ground cloves |
| 1 | tablespoon lemon juice | ¼ | cup brown sugar |
| 2 | teaspoons ground cinnamon | ½ | teaspoon vanilla extract |
| ¼ | teaspoon ground nutmeg | ¾ | cup apple juice |

## Crumb Topping

| | | | |
|---|---|---|---|
| ½ | cup (1 stick) butter, softened | ½ | teaspoon salt |
| ½ | cup all-purpose flour | ½ | teaspoon ground cinnamon |
| ½ | cup brown sugar | 1 | cup old-fashioned rolled oats |

1. Place diced apples in the insert of a multicooker. Add lemon juice, cinnamon, nutmeg, cloves, and sugar and toss apples to coat. Stir in vanilla and apple juice.

2. Prepare crumb topping: In a medium mixing bowl, combine butter, flour, brown sugar, salt, cinnamon, and oats with a fork or pastry cutter until a crumb-like texture forms.

3. Sprinkle topping over apple mixture in the multicooker insert, but do not stir.

4. Secure the lid and make sure the valve is pointing up to SEALING.

5. Press MANUAL (or press PRESSURE COOK and select HIGH PRESSURE) and adjust time to 1 minute.

6. When multicooker signals the end of cooking time, press CANCEL, and then quick release the pressure by turning the valve down to VENTING with the handle of a wooden spoon or other device to prevent the steam from burning your hands during the release.

7. Serve warm, topped with vanilla ice cream, if desired.

# APPLE PECAN MUFFINS

Prep time: 15 minutes | Pressurization and cooking time: 50 minutes | Total time: 1 hour 5 minutes | Yields: 6 muffins

| | | | |
|---|---|---|---|
| ¾ | cup all-purpose flour | 4 | tablespoons butter, softened |
| ½ | cup granulated sugar | ⅓ | cup milk |
| 1 | teaspoon baking soda | 2 | eggs |
| 1 | teaspoon baking powder | 1 | teaspoon vanilla extract |
| 1 | teaspoon ground cinnamon | ½ | gala apple, peeled and diced |
| ¼ | cup chopped pecans | 1½ | cups water |

## Streusel Topping

| | | | |
|---|---|---|---|
| ⅓ | cup brown sugar | ½ | teaspoon ground cinnamon |
| 1 | tablespoon all-purpose flour | 1 | tablespoon butter |

## Glaze

| | | | |
|---|---|---|---|
| ½ | cup powdered sugar | 1½ | tablespoons milk |
| 2 | tablespoons butter, melted | ¼ | teaspoon vanilla extract |

1. In a large mixing bowl, whisk together flour, sugar, baking soda, baking powder, cinnamon, and pecans.

2. In a separate bowl, mix together butter, milk, eggs, and vanilla. Stir into dry ingredients, then fold in diced apple pieces and set aside.

3. Prepare streusel topping: In a small bowl, stir together sugar, flour, and cinnamon. Use a fork or pastry cutter to blend in butter until small crumbs form.

4. Lightly spray 6 silicone muffin liners with nonstick cooking spray. Spoon batter into liners about ¾ full and top each with a generous spoonful of streusel topping.

5. Pour 1½ cups water in the insert of a multicooker. Place muffins on a 3-inch tall trivet and cover lightly with foil.

6. Carefully place trivet and covered muffins in the multicooker insert, secure the lid, and make sure the valve is pointing up to SEALING.

7. Press MANUAL (or press PRESSURE COOK and select HIGH PRESSURE) and adjust time to 25 minutes.

8. When multicooker signals the end of cooking time, let pressure naturally release 10 minutes and then carefully turn the valve to VENTING to quick release remaining pressure.

9. Remove lid, take off foil, and carefully transfer muffins from the multicooker to a wire cooling rack.

10. Prepare glaze: In a small bowl, combine sugar, melted butter, milk, and vanilla and stir until smooth. Drizzle glaze over cooled muffins and serve.

# PEACH COBBLER

Prep time: 10 minutes | Pressurization and cooking time: 40 minutes | Total time: 50 minutes | Yields: 6 servings

2 cups fresh or frozen sliced peaches

⅓ cup brown sugar

1 teaspoon ground cinnamon

1 cup water

1 cup boxed yellow cake mix

4 tablespoons cold butter, cut into thin slices

Vanilla ice cream or 1 cup freshly whipped cream, for garnishing

1. In a large mixing bowl, toss peaches with cinnamon and brown sugar until all the peaches are coated. Transfer peaches to a 7-inch round cake pan. Sprinkle cake mix over peaches to cover and layer sliced butter pieces over the cake mix. Cover pan loosely with aluminum foil.

2. Pour water in the insert of a multicooker and place trivet inside.

3. Carefully place pan on top of trivet in the multicooker insert, secure the lid, and make sure the valve is pointing up to SEALING.

4. Press MANUAL (or press PRESSURE COOK and select HIGH PRESSURE) and adjust time to 15 minutes.

5. When multicooker signals the end of cooking time, let pressure naturally release 10 minutes and then carefully turn the valve to VENTING to quick release remaining pressure.

6. Remove lid, carefully transfer pan from the multicooker insert to a wire rack, and take off foil.

7. Serve warm with a scoop of vanilla ice cream or freshly whipped cream.

# CHERRY DUMP CAKE

Prep time: 5 minutes | Pressurization and cooking time: 48 minutes | Total time: 52 minutes | Yields: 6 servings

2   (20-ounce) cans cherry pie filling

1   cup boxed yellow cake mix

4   tablespoons butter, thinly sliced

1   cup water

1   tablespoon granulated sugar

Vanilla ice cream or freshly whipped cream, for topping

1. Spray a 7-inch cake pan or springform pan with nonstick cooking spray. Pour cherry pie filling into the prepared pan and smooth out the top. Sprinkle cake mix over cherries to cover and layer sliced butter pieces over the cake mix. Cover pan with aluminum foil.

2. Pour water in the insert of a multicooker and place trivet inside.

3. Carefully place covered pan on top of trivet in the multicooker insert, secure the lid, and make sure the valve is pointing up to SEALING.

4. Press MANUAL (or press PRESSURE COOK and select HIGH PRESSURE) and adjust time to 25 minutes.

5. When multicooker signals the end of cooking time, let pressure naturally release 5 minutes and then carefully turn the valve to VENTING to quick release remaining pressure.

6. Remove lid, carefully transfer pan from the multicooker insert to a wire rack, and take off foil.

7. Heat oven broiler to high. Sprinkle cake with sugar and place under broiler until the top becomes crisp, about 3 minutes.

8. Serve warm with a scoop of vanilla ice cream or freshly whipped cream.

# SNICKERS CARAMEL POKE CAKE

Prep time: 15 minutes | Pressurization and cooking time: 1 hour | Total time: 1 hour 15 minutes, plus time to chill overnight | Yields: 8 servings

1  (15.25-ounce) package chocolate cake mix

Water, oil, and eggs called for on cake mix box

1  cup water

¾  cup caramel topping, divided

1  cup nondairy whipped topping, thawed

3  mini Snickers candy bars, chopped

1. Prepare cake batter according to directions on the box.

2. Spray a 7-inch springform pan with cooking spray and pour batter into it, making sure to leave 1/2 inch between the batter and top of the pan. Cover pan tightly with heavy duty aluminum foil.

3. Pour 1 cup water in the insert of a multicooker and place a trivet in insert.

4. Carefully place pan on top of trivet in the multicooker insert, secure the lid, and make sure the valve is pointing up to SEALING.

5. Press MANUAL (or press PRESSURE COOK and select HIGH PRESSURE) and adjust time to 45 minutes.

6. When multicooker signals the end of cooking time, press CANCEL, and then quick release the pressure by turning the valve down to VENTING with the handle of a wooden spoon or other device to prevent the steam from burning your hands during the release.

7. Remove lid, carefully transfer pan from the multicooker insert to a wire rack, and take off foil.

8. While cake is still hot, use the tines of a fork to poke holes in the cake every 1½ inches.

9. Drizzle ½ cup of the caramel topping evenly over the cake. (If caramel isn't thin enough to drizzle, heat it in a microwave-safe bowl 15 to 20 seconds to thin it out.) Let cake cool to room temperature, cover it with plastic wrap, and chill in the refrigerator overnight.

10. When ready to serve, use a serving plate to invert cake and then release the springform pan.

11. Spread whipped topping over cake, drizzle with remaining caramel, and top with chopped Snickers bars. Slice and serve.

# CHOCOLATE CHIP BANANA CAKE

Prep time: 20 minutes | Pressurization and cooking time: 1 hour 35 minutes | Total time: 1 hour 55 minutes | Yields: 8 servings

| | | | | |
|---|---|---|---|---|
| 1 | cup water | | 2 | eggs |
| 1¾ | cups all-purpose flour | | ½ | cup (1 stick) butter, melted |
| ¾ | cup granulated sugar | | ⅓ | cup milk |
| ½ | cup brown sugar | | 2 | teaspoons vanilla extract |
| 1 | teaspoon baking soda | | 3 | very ripe bananas, mashed |
| ½ | teaspoon salt | | 1½ | cups milk chocolate chips |
| 1 | teaspoon ground cinnamon | | | |

1. Pour 1 cup water in the insert of a multicooker and place trivet inside. Spray a 7-inch cake pan or springform pan with nonstick cooking spray and set aside.

2. In a large bowl, whisk together flour, sugars, baking soda, salt, and cinnamon. In a smaller bowl, whisk together eggs, melted butter, milk, and vanilla. With a wooden spoon, stir the wet mixture into the dry mixture until well combined. Add mashed bananas and stir. Fold in chocolate chips with a rubber spatula.

3. Spread batter into prepared pan. Using 2 square pieces of aluminum foil, cover the pan tightly.

4. Carefully place foil-covered pan on top of trivet in the multicooker insert, secure the lid, and make sure the valve is pointing up to SEALING.

5. Press MANUAL (or press PRESSURE COOK and select HIGH PRESSURE) and adjust time to 65 minutes.

6. When multicooker signals the end of cooking time, let pressure naturally release.

7. Remove lid, carefully transfer pan from the multicooker insert to a wire rack, and take off foil and paper towel. Invert bread onto a plate (or, if using a springform pan, release the sides), cut, and serve. This tastes especially good topped with whipped cream and a drizzle of caramel.

# CREAMY CHEESECAKE

Prep time: 15 minutes | Pressurization and cooking time: 1 hour 20 minutes | Total time: 1 hour 35 minutes, plus at least 6 hours chilling time in refrigerator | Yields: 8 servings

### Graham Cracker Crust

1   cup water

1   cup graham cracker crumbs

⅔   cup plus 1 tablespoon granulated sugar, divided

3   tablespoons butter, melted

### Cheesecake

2   (8-ounce) packages cream cheese, softened

1   teaspoon vanilla extract

½   teaspoon salt

2   eggs

Sliced strawberries, for topping

1. Pour 1 cup water in the insert of a multicooker and place trivet in the bottom of the insert. Spray a 7-inch springform pan with nonstick cooking spray and set aside.

2. In a small mixing bowl, combine graham cracker crumbs, 1 tablespoon of the sugar, and butter. Press mixture into the bottom and up the sides of the prepared springform pan. Set aside.

3. In the bowl of a stand mixer fitted with the paddle attachment, beat softened cream cheese until smooth, about 2 minutes. Beat in remaining ⅔ cup sugar, vanilla, salt, and eggs until smooth.

4. Pour mixture over graham cracker crust, smooth out the top, and cover pan tightly with foil.

5. Carefully place pan on top of trivet in the multicooker insert, secure the lid, and make sure the valve is pointing up to SEALING.

6. Press MANUAL (or press PRESSURE COOK and select HIGH PRESSURE) and adjust time to 35 minutes.

7. When multicooker signals the end of cooking time, let pressure naturally release 30 minutes and then carefully turn the valve to VENTING to quick release any remaining pressure.

8. Remove lid, carefully transfer pan from the multicooker insert to a wire rack, and take off foil.

9. Let cheesecake cool some before loosening the sides from the pan with a butter knife. Refrigerate at least 6 hours (or overnight).

10. Top with sliced strawberries before serving.

# KEY LIME PIE

Prep time: 15 minutes | Pressurization and cooking time: 40 minutes | Total time: 55 minutes | Yields: 6 to 8 servings

1 cup graham cracker crumbs

¼ cup butter, melted

3 tablespoons sugar, divided

4 egg yolks

⅔ cup key lime juice

1 tablespoon key lime zest, plus more for garnishing

1 (14-ounce) can sweetened condensed milk

⅓ cup sour cream

1 cup water

1 cup freshly whipped cream, for garnishing

Lime slices, for garnishing

1. Spray a 7-inch springform pan with nonstick cooking spray and set aside.

2. In a small mixing bowl, combine graham cracker crumbs, 1 tablespoon of the sugar, and butter. Press mixture into the bottom and up the sides of prepared pan. Place in freezer while preparing key lime filling.

3. In a large mixing bowl, whisk together egg yolks and remaining 2 tablespoons sugar until mixture turns a pale yellow. Add lime juice, zest, sweetened condensed milk, and sour cream and whisk until combined. Remove crust from freezer, pour key lime mixture into prepared crust, and cover with aluminum foil.

4. Pour 1 cup water in the insert of a multicooker and place trivet inside.

5. Carefully place foil covered springform pan on top of trivet in the multicooker insert, secure the lid, and make sure the valve is pointing up to SEALING.

6. Press MANUAL (or press PRESSURE COOK and select HIGH PRESSURE) and adjust time to 15 minutes.

7. When multicooker signals the end of cooking time, let pressure naturally release 10 minutes and then carefully turn the valve to VENTING to quick release remaining pressure.

8. Remove lid, carefully transfer pan from the multicooker insert to a wire rack, and take off foil.

9. Release sides from the springform pan and let pie cool to room temperature. Once cool, cover with plastic wrap and refrigerate 3 hours.

10. Serve, garnished with freshly whipped cream, lime wedges, and extra zest.

# DEEP-DISH DARK CHOCOLATE BROWNIE PIE

Prep time: 15 minutes | Pressurization and cooking time: 1 hour 10 minutes | Total time: 1 hour 25 minutes | Yields: 6 to 8 servings

½ **cup (1 stick) butter, softened**

1 **cup granulated sugar**

2 **eggs**

1 **teaspoon vanilla extract**

½ **cup unsweetened cocoa powder**

1 **teaspoon baking soda**

½ **teaspoon salt**

¾ **cup all-purpose flour**

1 **cup mini semisweet chocolate chips**

1½ **cups water**

1. In a large mixing bowl with an electric mixer, cream together butter and sugar until light and fluffy, about 2 minutes.

2. Add eggs and vanilla and mix until combined.

3. Add cocoa powder, baking soda, salt, and flour and mix on low speed until well combined.

4. With a rubber spatula, fold in mini chocolate chips.

5. Spray a 7-inch springform pan with nonstick cooking spray and transfer batter to pan, smoothing out the top with a spatula. Cover pan tightly with foil and set aside.

6. Pour 1½ cups water in the insert of a multicooker and place trivet in insert.

7. Carefully place foil-covered pan on top of trivet.

8. Secure the lid and make sure the valve is pointing up to SEALING.

9. Press MANUAL (or press PRESSURE COOK and select HIGH PRESSURE) and adjust time to 50 minutes.

10. When multicooker signals the end of cooking time, let pressure naturally release 10 minutes and then carefully turn the valve to VENTING to quick release remaining pressure.

11. Remove lid and carefully transfer pan to a wire rack to cool.

12. Once cool, slice into wedges and serve.

# FUDGY BROWNIES

Prep time: 10 minutes | Pressurization and cooking time: 1 hour 15 minutes | Total time: 1 hour 25 minutes | Yields: 10 brownies

---

½ cup (1 stick) butter, softened

1 cup granulated sugar

2 eggs

1½ teaspoons vanilla extract

¾ cup all-purpose flour

⅓ cup unsweetened cocoa powder

½ teaspoon baking powder

¼ teaspoon salt

1 cup semi-sweet chocolate chips

½ cup chopped walnuts

1. In a large bowl, beat softened butter with a hand mixer for 10 seconds; add sugar and mix until well blended. Beat in eggs, add vanilla, and mix again.

2. In a separate bowl, whisk together flour, cocoa, baking powder, and salt. Add the dry ingredients to the wet mixture and stir by hand with a wooden spoon. Fold in the chocolate chips and walnuts.

3. Lightly spray a 7-inch springform pan with cooking spray. Spread the batter into the pan and smooth out the top. Cover with aluminum foil.

4. Place trivet in the insert of a multicooker and pour in 1 1/2 cups of water.

5. Carefully place foil-covered pan on top of trivet in the multicooker insert, secure the lid, and make sure the valve is pointing up to SEALING.

6. Place the lid on the multicooker and lock into place. Turn valve to SEALING. Push MANUAL or PRESSURE COOK and set timer for 55 minutes.

7. When multicooker signals the end of cooking time, let pressure naturally release 10 minutes and then carefully turn the valve to VENTING to quick release remaining pressure.

8. Remove lid, carefully transfer pan from the multicooker insert to a wire rack, and take off foil.

9. Let brownies cool in pan 15 minutes before releasing sides of springform pan. Slice into wedges and serve warm with ice cream.

# DEEP-DISH CHOCOLATE CHIP COOKIE

Prep time: 15 minutes | Pressurization and cooking time: 1 hour 15 minutes | Total time: 1 hour 30 minutes | Yields: 6 to 8 servings

½ cup (1 stick) unsalted butter, softened

⅓ cup granulated sugar

⅓ cup brown sugar

½ tablespoon vanilla extract

1 large egg

1⅔ cups all-purpose flour

½ teaspoon baking soda

½ teaspoon salt

1 cup milk chocolate chips

1½ cups water

Vanilla ice cream, for topping

Chocolate syrup, for topping

1. In the bowl of a stand mixer fitted with the paddle attachment, cream together butter and sugars until light and fluffy, about 2 minutes. Add vanilla and egg and mix until combined. Slowly mix in flour, baking soda, and salt, then fold in chocolate chips and stir until combined.

2. Spray a 7-inch springform pan with nonstick cooking spray and spread dough inside pan. Cover tightly with foil and set aside.

3. Pour 1½ cups water in the insert of a multicooker and place trivet inside.

4. Carefully place pan on top of trivet in the multicooker insert, secure the lid, and make sure the valve is pointing up to SEALING.

5. Press MANUAL (or press PRESSURE COOK and select HIGH PRESSURE) and adjust time to 50 minutes.

6. When multicooker signals the end of cooking time, let pressure naturally release 10 minutes and then carefully turn the valve to VENTING to quick release remaining pressure.

7. Remove lid, carefully transfer pan from the multicooker insert to a wire rack, and take off foil.

8. Let cookie cool slightly before slicing; serve warm, topped with vanilla ice cream and chocolate syrup.

# MULTICOOKER CHOCOLATE FUDGE

Prep time: 5 minutes | Pressurization and cooking time: 10 minutes | Total time: 15 minutes, plus 3 hours to set up | Yields: 25 (1.5-inch) pieces fudge

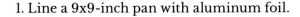

1   tablespoon butter

2   cups semi-sweet chocolate chips

1   (14-ounce) can sweetened condensed milk

Dash salt

1   teaspoon vanilla extract

1   (4.4-ounce) Hershey's milk chocolate candy bar, broken into small pieces

1. Line a 9x9-inch pan with aluminum foil.

2. Add butter to the insert of a multicooker and press SAUTÉ. After butter has melted, press CANCEL.

3. Add chocolate chips, sweetened condensed milk, salt, and vanilla and stir until chocolate chips have melted completely. Stir in candy bar pieces until melted.

4. Pour melted chocolate into prepared pan and refrigerate at least 3 hours to set.

5. Cut into 25 pieces and serve. Store in an airtight container in the refrigerator for up to 2 weeks.

# CHOCOLATE FONDUE

Prep time: 10 minutes | Pressurization and cooking time: 10 minutes | Total time: 20 minutes | Yields: 12 servings

2   cups water

1   (12-ounce) bag semi-sweet chocolate chips

1   cup milk chocolate chips

1   cup heavy cream

1   teaspoon vanilla extract

Dash salt

Sliced strawberries, banana slices, pineapple chunks, graham crackers, marshmallows, brownies, cinnamon bears, pretzels, and so on, for dipping

1. Pour 2 cups water into the insert of a multicooker. Place trivet in insert and then place a glass bowl with a lip on top of the trivet. (The lip will give you something to grab onto with oven mitts when you remove the bowl from the multicooker after finishing off the fondue.)

2. Place chocolate chips, cream, vanilla, and salt in the bowl. Press SAUTÉ. As the water heats up, occasionally stir the chocolate and cream. When chocolate begins to melt, continue stirring until chocolate is smooth, 8 to 10 minutes. Once chocolate is completely melted, press CANCEL and then press KEEP WARM.

3. Serve straight from the multicooker, stirring occasionally, so chocolate remains smooth. Use forks or skewers to dip fruit and sweets in the chocolate.

# DULCE DE LECHE CARAMEL

Prep time: 2 minutes | Pressurization and cooking time: 55 minutes | Total time: 57 minutes, plus cooling time | Yields: 1 (14-ounce) serving

**1 (14-ounce) can sweetened condensed milk (see note)**

**8 to 9 cups water, or more, depending on size of multicooker**

**1 teaspoon vanilla extract**

1. Remove the label and lid from the can of condensed milk. Cover the top of the open can with aluminum foil. Add trivet to the insert of a multicooker, place foil-wrapped can of condensed milk on top of trivet, and pour water around the can halfway up.

2. Secure the lid and make sure the valve is pointing up to SEALING.

3. Press MANUAL (or press PRESSURE COOK and select HIGH PRESSURE) and adjust time to 40 minutes.

4. When multicooker signals the end of cooking time, press CANCEL, and then quick release the pressure by turning the valve down to VENTING with the handle of a wooden spoon or other device to prevent the steam from burning your hands during the release.

5. Remove lid, carefully transfer pan from the multicooker insert to the countertop, and take off foil. Let cool 20 minutes. You'll see it will have transformed from ordinary condensed milk into a beautiful caramel Dulce de Leche.

6. After 20 minutes have passed, add vanilla right into the can and stir well for 2 minutes, until mixture goes from a lumpy consistency to a creamy one. Store in an airtight container in the refrigerator for up to 3 weeks.

*Note: You can make 2 or 3 cans at once in the multicooker; no need to adjust the cooking time. Just be sure to add 2 teaspoons vanilla to each can.*

# SOFT MONKEY BREAD

Prep time: 10 minutes, plus 2 hours thawing time | Pressurization and cooking time: 45 minutes | Total time: 2 hours 55 minutes, plus 4 hours rising time | Yields: 6 to 8 servings

---

16    **Rhodes frozen dinner rolls**

½    **cup chopped pecans**

1    **(3.5-ounce) package cook and serve butterscotch pudding**

½    **cup brown sugar**

6    **tablespoons butter, melted**

1. Place frozen rolls in a gallon-sized zipper top bag, seal bag, and let rolls thaw 1½ to 2 hours in bag. Do not let dough begin to rise.

2. Spray a 7-inch Bundt pan with nonstick cooking spray. (See note.) Scatter pecans in the bottom of the Bundt pan. In a small bowl, stir together brown sugar and melted butter.

3. Remove rolls from bag and cut each roll into 6 pieces using kitchen shears. Arrange half of the cut rolls over pecans and drizzle half of the sugar-butter mixture over rolls. Sprinkle half of the dry pudding mix over rolls.

4. Repeat with remaining rolls, sugar-butter mixture, and pudding mix.

5. Cover with plastic wrap that has been sprayed with nonstick cooking spray and let rise in the refrigerator 4 to 8 hours, until double in size.

6. When ready to bake, remove plastic wrap from the rolls, cover the pan with foil, and place 1 cup of water and then the pan in the insert of a multicooker.

7. Secure the lid and make sure the valve is pointing up to SEALING.

8. Press MANUAL (or press PRESSURE COOK and select HIGH PRESSURE) and adjust time to 30 minutes.

9. When multicooker signals the end of cooking time, press CANCEL, and then quick release the pressure by turning the valve down to VENTING with the handle of a wooden spoon or other device to prevent the steam from burning your hands during the release.

10. Remove lid and carefully transfer pan from the multicooker insert to a wire rack. Let cool 5 minutes then invert pan onto a plate so the butterscotch sauce and pecans are on the top of the monkey bread.

11. Serve warm.

*Note: If you don't have a Bundt pan, you can use stackable pans, such as Ekovana Stackable Insert Pans. If you use stackable pans, split ingredients between pans instead of layering on top of each other.*

# BREAD PUDDING

Prep time: 15 minutes | Pressurization and cooking time: 55 minutes | Total time: 1 hour 10 minutes | Yields: 4 to 6 servings

## Bread Pudding

1½   cups water

8   cups day-old cinnamon swirl bread, cut or torn into cubes

½   cup raisins

1½   cups half and half

3   eggs

1   teaspoon vanilla extract

½   cup granulated sugar

¼   teaspoon ground cinnamon

    Pinch salt

2   tablespoons butter, melted

## Caramel Sauce

½   cup heavy cream

½   cup brown sugar

½   cup light corn syrup

1. Pour 1½ cups water in the insert of a multicooker and place steamer basket inside. Spray 7-inch cake pan or springform pan with nonstick cooking spray.

2. In a large bowl, toss together dry bread cubes and raisins; set aside.

3. In a separate bowl, whisk together half and half, eggs, vanilla, sugar, cinnamon, salt, and melted butter. Pour mixture over the dry bread cubes and gently toss to mix, until the bread cubes are coated.

4. Spoon coated bread cubes into prepared cake pan, then press them down gently. Spray one side of aluminum foil with nonstick cooking spray, and cover the pan, sprayed side down, with foil.

5. Carefully place pan on top of steamer rack in the multicooker insert, secure the lid, and make sure the valve is pointing up to SEALING.

6. Press MANUAL (or press PRESSURE COOK and select HIGH PRESSURE) and adjust time to 30 minutes.

7. When multicooker signals the end of cooking time, let pressure naturally release 10 minutes and then carefully turn the valve to VENTING to quick release remaining pressure.

8. Remove lid and carefully transfer pan from the multicooker insert to a wire rack. Let pudding rest 5 minutes to cool slightly, then remove the foil.

9. Prepare caramel sauce: In a small saucepan over medium heat, stir together cream, sugar, and corn syrup until sugar is dissolved and mixture is warm and caramel-colored, about 6–8 minutes.

10. Serve the bread pudding with warm caramel sauce poured over the top.

# CHURRO BITES

Prep time: 10 minutes | Pressurization and cooking time: 36 minutes | Total time: 46 minutes | Yields: 10 churro bites

---

| | |
|---|---|
| 1 cup dry yellow cake mix | ½ teaspoon ground nutmeg |
| ⅓ cup water | 2½ teaspoons ground cinnamon, divided |
| 1 egg | ⅓ cup brown sugar |
| 2 tablespoons vegetable oil | |

1. Lightly spray 2 multicooker-safe silicone egg bites molds with nonstick cooking spray and set aside.

2. In a medium bowl, stir together cake mix, water, egg, and vegetable oil. Add nutmeg and 1 teaspoon of the cinnamon and mix until combined.

3. Spoon the cake batter into each cup of the egg bites molds, filling each ¾ full. Tap the molds gently on the counter to settle the batter and remove any air bubbles. Gently cover each mold loosely with foil and seal the edges.

4. Pour 1 cup water in the insert of a multicooker and place trivet inside.

5. Carefully lay the first egg bites mold on the trivet, then stack the second mold on top of the first, offsetting them slightly so they don't sink into each other.

6. Secure the lid and make sure the valve is pointing up to SEALING.

7. Press MANUAL (or press PRESSURE COOK and select HIGH PRESSURE) and adjust time to 11 minutes.

8. When multicooker signals the end of cooking time, let pressure naturally release 10 minutes and then carefully turn the valve to VENTING to quick release remaining pressure.

9. Remove lid, carefully transfer egg bites molds to countertop, and take off foil. Let churro bites rest 5 minutes.

10. In a small bowl, mix together brown sugar and remaining 1½ teaspoons cinnamon. Roll each churro bite in the mixture while they are still warm. Place churro bites on serving platter and enjoy!

# CANDIED ALMONDS

Prep time: 10 minutes | Pressurization and cooking time: 35 minutes | Total time: 45 minutes | Yields: 8 (½-cup) servings

| | | | | |
|---|---|---|---|---|
| 4 | cups almonds | ½ | teaspoon ground nutmeg |
| 1 | tablespoon butter | ½ | teaspoon salt |
| ½ | cup maple syrup | ½ | cup water |
| 1½ | teaspoons vanilla extract | ¼ | cup brown sugar |
| 1½ | teaspoons ground cinnamon | ¼ | cup granulated sugar |

1. Place almonds, butter, maple syrup, vanilla, cinnamon, nutmeg, and salt in the insert of a multicooker.

2. Press SAUTÉ and toss ingredients with a wooden spoon to coat almonds and melt butter, about 2–3 minutes. Add ½ cup water, stir again, and press CANCEL.

3. Secure the lid and make sure the valve is pointing up to SEALING.

4. Press MANUAL (or press PRESSURE COOK and select HIGH PRESSURE) and adjust time to 10 minutes.

5. When multicooker begins counting down the time, preheat the oven to 400 degrees F. and line a baking sheet with aluminum foil; set aside.

6. When multicooker signals the end of cooking time, press CANCEL, and then quick release the pressure by turning the valve down to VENTING with the handle of a wooden spoon or other device to prevent the steam from burning your hands during the release.

7. Remove lid and spoon almonds into a gallon-sized zipper-top bag. Add sugars to the bag, seal the bag, and shake to coat almonds.

8. Spread almonds on prepared baking sheet and roast 10 minutes, flipping almonds halfway through.

9. Serve warm or cool completely and store in an airtight container up to 7 days.

# STRAWBERRY JAM

Prep time: 10 minutes | Pressurization and cooking time: 35 minutes | Total time: 45 minutes | Yields: Makes 1⅛ cups jam

1   **pound fresh strawberries, washed and
    sliced**

2   **tablespoons granulated sugar**

2   **tablespoons freshly squeezed orange
    juice**

1. Place sliced strawberries in the insert of a
   multicooker and sprinkle sugar over the top.
   Allow berries to sit 10 to 15 minutes so the
   sugar macerates them. Pour freshly squeezed
   orange juice over the strawberries and sugar.

2. Secure the lid and make sure the valve is
   pointing up to SEALING.

3. Press MANUAL (or press PRESSURE COOK
   and select HIGH PRESSURE) and adjust time
   to 1 minute.

4. When multicooker signals the end of
   cooking time, let pressure naturally release
   15 minutes and then carefully turn the valve
   to VENTING to quick release remaining
   pressure.

5. Carefully remove lid and use a potato masher
   to crush berries.

6. Transfer mixture to a 16-ounce jar or
   small bowl to cool. It will thicken up as it
   cools. Store in an airtight container in the
   refrigerator up to 2 weeks.

# APPLE CIDER

Prep time: 10 minutes | Pressurization and cooking time: 30 minutes | Total time: 40 minutes | Yields: 8 (1-cup) servings

7 medium apples, such as Granny Smith and gala, quartered

1 orange, peeled and quartered

½ cup fresh cranberries

½ cup granulated sugar

2 cinnamon sticks

½ teaspoon whole cloves

Water to cover fruit

1. Place the cut apples, orange wedges, and cranberries in the insert of a multicooker. Add sugar, cinnamon sticks, and whole cloves on top and pour in enough water to cover the fruit.

2. Secure the lid and make sure the valve is pointing up to SEALING.

3. Press MANUAL (or press PRESSURE COOK and select HIGH PRESSURE) and adjust time to 15 minutes.

4. When multicooker signals the end of cooking time, press CANCEL, and then quick release the pressure by turning the valve down to VENTING with the handle of a wooden spoon or other device to prevent the steam from burning your hands during the release.

5. Remove lid and mash the fruit with a potato masher to release more juices and flavor.

6. Carefully drain the solids from the liquids with a fine mesh sieve; discard the solids.

7. Serve warm. Store the cider in an airtight container up to 1 week in the refrigerator.

# HOT CHOCOLATE

Prep time: 5 minutes | Pressurization and cooking time: 22 minutes | Total time: 27 minutes | Yields: 6 (8-ounce) servings

½   cup unsweetened cocoa powder

½   cup granulated sugar

½   teaspoon ground cinnamon

¼   teaspoon salt

4   cups milk

1   teaspoon vanilla extract

Mini marshmallows, freshly whipped cream, or crushed candy canes, for garnishing

1. Add cocoa powder, sugar, cinnamon, salt, milk, and vanilla to the insert of a multicooker and whisk until smooth.

2. Secure the lid and make sure the valve is pointing up to SEALING.

3. Press MANUAL (or press PRESSURE COOK and select HIGH PRESSURE) and adjust time to 2 minutes.

4. When multicooker signals the end of cooking time, let pressure naturally release 5 minutes and then carefully turn the valve to VENTING to quick release remaining pressure.

5. Remove lid, whisk, and serve, garnished with marshmallows, whipped cream, or crushed candy canes.

# INFUSED PEACH-RASPBERRY LEMONADE

Prep time: 10 minutes | Pressurization and cooking time: 20 minutes | Total time: 30 minutes | Yields: Enough concentrate to make 10 (12-ounce) servings

| | |
|---|---|
| **1** cup chopped peaches | **4 to 5** cups water |
| **½** cup raspberries | **Zest and juice of 1 lemon** |

1. Place fruit in a mesh steamer basket and set basket in the insert of a multicooker. Add lemon zest, juice, and enough water to barely cover the fruit.

2. Secure the lid and make sure the valve is pointing up to SEALING.

3. Press MANUAL (or press PRESSURE COOK and select HIGH PRESSURE) and adjust time to 5 minutes.

4. When multicooker signals the end of cooking time, press CANCEL, and then quick release the pressure by turning the valve down to VENTING with the handle of a wooden spoon or other device to prevent the steam from burning your hands during the release.

5. Remove lid carefully and, using a wooden spoon, lightly mash the cooked fruit to release some juice into the insert, then carefully lift out basket of fruit, and discard fruit.

6. Let the flavored water cool slightly in the multicooker insert and then pour into a mason jar, top with a pourable lid, and place in the refrigerator to chill.

7. To serve, add 2 to 3 tablespoons of the concentrate to 8 ounces cold water, stir, and enjoy. If desired, you can stir in honey or sugar to sweeten the drink.

*Note: You can also freeze the infused water in an ice cube tray and pop cubes into your bottled water for a flavorful drink on the go.*

# index

Page references in *italics* indicate photographs.